CW01590195

ANCHOR BOOKS

FUNNY THAT!

Edited by

Rachael Radford

First published in Great Britain in 2003 by
ANCHOR BOOKS
Remus House,
Coltsfoot Drive,
Peterborough, PE2 9JX
Telephone (01733) 898102

All Rights Reserved

Copyright Contributors 2003

HB ISBN 1 84418 128 6
SB ISBN 1 84418 129 4

FOREWORD

Anchor Books is a small press, established in 1992, with the aim of promoting readable poetry to as wide an audience as possible.

We hope to establish an outlet for writers of poetry who may have struggled to see their work in print.

The poems presented here have been selected from many entries, and as always editing proved to be a difficult task.

I trust this selection will delight and please the authors and all those who enjoy reading poetry.

Rachael Radford
Editor

CONTENTS

GARDEN GNOMES

Garden gnomes, I hate the things
ugly little brutes,
All short and squat, and beards and feet,
and stupid, rosy cheeks.

They sit all day by garden ponds,
with fishing rods in their hands,
Gazing blankly into space,
and never catch a thing.

They lurk around on rockeries,
and in the flower beds.
Some with wheelbarrows, some on swings,
and some just standing there.

Garden gnomes, I hate the things
ugly little brutes,
I wish someone would be so kind
and come and steal my dads.

Then I could sunbathe on the lawn,
in privacy at last.
Without those beady little eyes
watching every move.

Sheila Giles

THE SOLICITOR

He walks in the centre of the city,
Bowler hat on head, briefcase in hand,
And makes his way along The Strand
Till he comes to the office door.

Very carefully, he unlocks it,
Pushes it open wide,
Peeps round the corner to make sure it's safe,
Then quickly steps inside.

He takes off his hat and hangs it up,
At his desk he seats himself
And soon he is confronted
With a lady of much wealth.

He hasn't yet proved his worth in law
And with an upward glance,
When she asks him for his help,
He hopes this is his chance.

As he thinks he's gained a client,
Who is it he should see,
But his superior, who says to him,
'Ernest, go and make the tea.'

Joyce Walker

DIY

My attempts at DIY,
Usually end with my temper high,
A hole in the wall, twice as big as it should,
Instead of a plank, a pile of match wood.
Screws will not screw
And nails seem to bend
Although I can hit them
On the right end.

Give me some wool
And a pattern with cables.
I'll knit you a jersey
As quick as I'm able.
Or some silk and a pattern
For a dress, very swish
And I'll have it done
As quick as you wish.
So it does puzzle me
And I cry why oh why
Am I so D-I-M
at DIY.

Joan Gray

EMPTINESS

My heart is full of sorrow;
My spirit, full of woe.
All my feelings have gone numb,
I don't know where to go.

How can life be so cruel,
So shameless and so hard?
Why is it always little me
Who's dealt the losing card?

How can this really happen,
At my favourite drinking ground;
When the money's ready in my hand
To pay for the first round?

I'm thirsty, dry - and sober;
So happy to be here.
But, now they've just informed me
That the pub's run out of beer!

Brian M Wood

A Fistful Of Prayers . . .

All was quiet in the church,
It was scarcely dawn,
Preparing for the weekly service
As we did each Sunday morn.

Sacred vessels on the altar,
The candles all a-flicker,
Waiting for the congregation
And the arrival of the vicar.

Outside the sky was heavy,
The rain was pouring down,
When through the creaking door appeared
Neville in his long, black gown.

On his head he wore a hat -
Much more effective than a hood -
It kept him dry, but made him look
Like a clerical Clint Eastwood!

Carol Anne Edwards

Then You Go And Spoil It All

You cook us a romantic dinner
Just for two
Then you go and spoil it all
By saying your mother
Did the cooking for you
Then we sit down to a romantic film
That I have rented
Then you go and spoil it all
By telling me how it ended
Then there upon the bed you lay
A playful smile upon your lips
You beckon me to come and play
With your arms outstretched
Then you close your eyes
And I do that thing
That drives you wild and insane
Then I go and spoil it all
By calling out your mother's name

Philip Robertson

Problem Solved

I think I ought to write this down
I'm not much of a talker
But something strange is going on -
It seems I have a 'Stalker'!
He doesn't phone, he doesn't write
But I know he's always there,
Keeping in the background,
Turning up, just everywhere!

I find I'm going places now
I've never thought of going,
Just to keep him occupied
Without him really knowing.
We've been to all the restaurants -
We've joined some expeditions -
Visited the ballet -
Queued up for exhibitions.

Now something else is happening,
I couldn't really swear it
But my Stalker has a 'Stalker'
There's three of us to share it!
I'm running out of where to go
So I have a cunning plot -
If I play my cards right
I can soon sort out this lot!

I'll just become a 'Stalker' too;
Instead of being friendless,
Although they'll never know it,
Our future now is endless!

Pat Watson

A Bit Of A Day

Young Bill was happy at his desk, no stress to mar his day
Until he raised the telephone - heard wife Terina say
'Don't worry dear, your baby's safe, I have her in the car
We're sitting here awaiting help, my oven is on fire.'

He drove along the road at speed, too reckless for his liking
And saw a sign - Drive carefully, the firemen are striking!
On reaching home, a cul-de-sac, he found he couldn't enter
Fire engines, three complete with crews, his kitchen at the centre.

The neighbours out, the cameras too, recording such reaction
His blushing wife aware that fairy cakes had caused the action
The sign upon the motorway he felt that it should say -
My wife has all the firemen - drive carefully today!

Dorothy Blakeman

The Homecoming

I forgot the flowers, they're dead in their vase.
My bum's gone numb, I've been driving for hours.
The house is cold and it smells musty,
The bread in the bin has gone all crusty.
I forgot the milk and I hate black tea,
According to 1571, the phone's rung constantly.
The mail's ankle deep and there'll be nothing good,
I emptied the fridge so I know there's no food,
The boiler's gone out, so bang goes the heat.
My shoes are too tight and they're killing my feet.
There's something unpleasant been left in the bin,
It's all too depressing, thank God I've got gin.
My stomach is growling, they're doing DIY in my head.
I'll just have another, then I'm off to bed.
I've looked out to the garden, someone's stolen my gnome,
In spite of all this, I'm quite glad to be home.

Pamela Matthews

FUNNY SIDE

To teach me to dance
When I could only prance
Was the job of Sarah Jane
Who lived down the lane
'Two left feet!' sez she to me
With that I had to agree.
She had patience, no end
And she didn't pretend
That I was easy to steer
From there to here.
'Your timing's so bad'
She says 'it's just sad.'
'But I have never failed yet
So I'll make you a bet
That waltz you will do
In one year or two.'
I looked with a grin
And me just all in.
Thinking will my two feet
Then look so neat
When I waltz with great grace
And keep up the pace.
Will Sarah Jane then say
'Let's call it a day
A work of art to my name
I sure will achieve fame.
I'll retire with a smile
And rest for a while
Goodbye to you, pupil -
You never were supple.'

Brigid O'Donnell

Swimming

I can do front stroke, back stroke
Doggy paddle and all.
From here in my armchair over
To the wall.
S'pose I really oughta
Try it in the water!

Clare Todd

The Vow Of Silence

The young monks in the Abbey sat
They knew that there would be no chat
To keep the silence they had vowed
Only two words every seven years allowed

For seven years Tarman toiled and prayed
All the rules he had obeyed
The two words he had carefully chose
So he said 'bed hard' as he arose

The years went by, until at last
Another seven years had passed
Tarman came to the Abbot and the Abbot was told
In a firm fervent voice 'food cold'

The years dragged by, seven more
Tarman came to the Abbot, looking sore
His two words rang throughout the room
'I quit' but then he heard the Abbot boom
'Shut up, you're always complaining.'

Joan Magennis

SHOWDOWN

Two ageing gangland heavyweights
Squared up outside a pub
Their best days now behind them
On account of too much grub

A shot rang out, a wounded shout
One lurched towards the other
A heavy price to pay
For chatting up the other's lover

The first hood tried to step aside
A matter of survival
Suffice to say
In their own way
Both found 'dead on a rival'

Gordon A Hobbs

Gift Wrapped

The new man in me, at last recognising there is a changed woman in
my life, blurts out, 'I'll wrap the Christmas presents dear, it's high
time I did my stint.'
'Thank you honey, you'll need some bandages and lint,' says my
supportive wife.
'I'll pop out to the chemist, get you some blunt scissors, top up
the first aid kit. Will a dozen bin bags be enough for the off-cuts?
I'm sure there'll be a mint.'
'Oh, can it Sarah. You should know by now, sarcasm is the lowest
form of wit.'

I'm starting off the Sellotape: it's like chasing your own tail - you're
bound to fail; This is the way my little world begins: not with a bang
but an abject whimper: if it starts at all. Pick away; I'm turning grey;
I don't get this with my e-mail! I yelp as I break another nail.
'All right dear?' Sarah looks in with an *I told you so* simper.
This is hopeless: 'Sarah, get me a bloody cutlass and a quart of my
home-brewed ale.' I cry as I slash at the roll with a kitchen knife:
for by now I'm in a terrible temper.

Eight inch long pieces now stick insanely to my extended fingers
and thumbs, like yellow hostage ribbons for taped-up, bin-bagged
victims come to grief.
A plague on all their houses, with their inanely unsympathetic gums;
and just how can I get rid of that annoying piece stuck to my bottom
teeth? At last some ragged parcels lie crudely wrapped around my
feathered feet, festooned with scraps of scissored paper and savagely
bitten adhesive tape.

I shuffle round with faltering steps, my face mottled, red as a boiled-up
beet, until two exhausting days have passed and I can finally make my
escape. And now, beneath the decorated tree, hidden by off-cuts from
my wrapping paper, lies a grotty grotto of lumpy apologies for
gift-wrapped Christmas presents; busy capturing passing insects like
sticky strips of arsenicated fly-paper, where late sacrificial winter
wasps impart a festive and buzzing radiance.

Unwrapping time at last: a frenzied group of ripping, clawing, guests
tears into my Fort Knox of parcels, like an ill-trained chainsaw team,
soon sporting sticky yellow hostage ribbons on their chins and chests,
until at last they all grow tired of letting off so much useless steam.
Then ma-in-law reveals a tube of scented 'Strongjaw' shaving cream,
while pa-in-law unwraps a year's supply of her Browning Bisto;
my wife receives a model train that runs on super-pressurised steam;
Aunty May, a full-sized sex-shop blow-up of the Count of Monte
Christo. They all try to exchange their gifts: an earring for a Barbie doll:
jig-saw puzzle for garden trowel, Chanel No 5 for Oil of Wintergreen.
But all knew of my suffering and how it had taken its horrendous toll,
smiling in embarrassment as I unwrap - my fifteenth Sellotape machine!

Norman Meadows

THE COFFIN DODGERS

Look out for the Coffin Dodgers
Whilst walking in the street,
If they've got time to stop and talk,
You're in for such a treat.

No longer do they stagger past
With Zimmer frame in hand,
More often they'll be dancing out late
With the local band.

Gone are the days of purple rinse,
Men's noses stained with snuff,
You'll find these golden oldies
Are made of sterner stuff.

Swimming, cycling, jogging too,
Lots of things to learn and do.
Opportunities galore,
Get out there and do some more.

But then some days they get up
And are feeling all washed out.
Their muscles ache and joints swell up,
Could be a touch of gout.

Time to relax and take time out,
Reflect on how life's been,
The friends they've made,
Things they've done and places they have seen.

They must not get disheartened
When life seems far from cool,
Just remember these few precious words,
The Coffin Dodgers rule!

Julie Brewer

Don't You Just Love 'Em?

Disputes with a loved one, never is easy,
He wants a sweet dish . . . you . . . something cheesy.
He's strong and silent, you want to talk,
He takes the car when you'd rather walk.
Friends you've known ages, he says they're bores,
You fancy shopping, he says, 'do chores.'
'What's all this reading and sewing and knitting?'
'Get a life girl, I'm going fishing.'
'Make-up? Don't bother, we won't be out long.'
'You make such a fuss, you know I'm not wrong.'
'Me? Need a shave? Oh give it a rest.
Next you'll be saying, wear a clean vest.'
They need understanding, these overgrown boys,
The biggest difference . . . the price of their toys.
As they grow up, they cost such a lot
And just a much use as a chocolate teapot.
Defensive when challenged, they think it's a thrill,
But the little boy's still there if ever they're ill!
I think we should change, where roles are reversed,
Partnership's hard, we should have rehearsed.
Take heart, he'll see your side, if just now and then,
We must make allowances . . . they're only *men*,
But girls though they make us all rant, rave and bawl,
Don't we just love 'em? . . . Their warts and all!
And today, so lovingly holding my hand,
He told me I'm complex to understand.

Janet Dow

MURPHY

My best mate is one Murphy by name,
His long nose and big ears are truly of fame.
Wherever he goes, he leaves in disgrace,
Wrecked gardens, dirty clothes, are always in place.
He once ate someone's hat and damaged her door,
Now and again he leaves her a present, on the floor.
He loves to drive around in posh motorcars,
Signing his autograph just like the stars.
His hair is too long, he's really a scruff
And he'll finish your glass when he sees you've had enough.
I must take him to meet the Queen,
She would forget all her corgis with my Murphy's beam.
She could feed him caviar and foods of the best,
He would even eat biscuits when put to the test,
But don't show him a cat or he will turn into a dog,
Barking and woofing, till you pray to God
And when it's all over, he just wags his tail,
For you are responsible and must now pay his bail.
If I didn't love him, I'd kill him quite dead,
But he's my mate Murphy and needs to be fed.

Les Allen

THE CHICKENS AND THE SUPERMARKET

The chickens in the car park are causing quite a row,
For years they've roosted in the hedges and foraged 'neath the trees
And pecked around the village shop, as saucy as you please -
But where are they to go to? And what will happen now

That Multicheap the Supermart will build upon this site?
Instead of chickens scratching, there'll be shelves and shelves of tins
And stacks and stacks of biscuits - the thick ones and the thins
Forming psychedelic patterns, because they're packed so tight.

The chickens cluck contentedly - they don't know what's to come,
For Planning smiles approvingly on Multicheap's request
And looks with umbrage at the poultry, considered just a pest,
With chicks busy hatching in the springtime and cheeping at their mum.

But Management says, 'No worries, we've got a plan you see,
The plan includes the chickens, it's on the drawing board.
They'll live their lives in luxury - that's what we can afford,
Don't ask too many questions or you'll have them for your tea.'

The villagers are up in arms, the chickens must remain:
They got there first, it is their patch, the car park is their run -
Pecking daintily among the cars and roosting at the setting of the sun,
And Multicheap can go *** elsewhere, their supermart's a pain.

The diggers and the builders' trucks arrive one freezing dawn
And meet a line of villagers - not thin, not blue, but deep;
The protectors of the poultry, who sacrificed their sleep
To save the car park for the chickens on that dark portentous morn.

Rosemary Harvey

THE PARTY NIGHT OUT

He dressed up as a bear
They had to go where?
Of course, to a fancy dress party
He felt so hot, when at last he was ready

So, off he went, with his late wife so trim
Now I will tell you what happened to him
As I put this in rhyme
They got there before time

Quite a number of people were late
For this fancy dress party date
And all dressed in suits, hats and tie
He felt so embarrassed, and felt, he just wanted to fly

They had to stay there till midnight
Oh my, he really did look quite a sight
They all watched him with humour
And bent over with laughter

He couldn't take his head off, for the need of a cigar
Through this event, that did occur
He was helped to drink, from a straw
And certainly couldn't eat, what's more

He could not take the costume off at all
He would even so have looked more of a fool
For he only had his underwear on
To stay, till the party was over and done

When they arrived home, he felt so hot and stuffy
The bear's costume came off in a jiffy
It made him feel a right a right banana
And was glad when the party was over

Now he can laugh at this humorous past
But will never attempt to dress up, as a bear so fast.

Jean McGovern

CONFUSED

I am a little dickie bird
Sitting in a cage,
I never lose my temper
Or get into a rage.
I sit and sing, then preen myself,
My feathers all in place,
I look into my mirror
And see my little face,
Then a voice outside my cage says,
'Who's a pretty boy?'
My master's always saying that,
I wonder, *why, what for?*
That's just too much, I can't say that,
I feel a little surly,
She obviously hasn't noticed,
I am a little 'girlie.'

Elsie Kemp

The Empty Rocking Chair

The old rocking chair stands empty today,
For Grandmama's no longer in it.
She's off in her car down the wide motorway;
She buzzes around every minute.

You won't find her slipping off early to bed
From her chair in a warm chimney nook.
Her computer is tapping far into the night,
For Grandma is writing a book.

Our Grandmama never allows backward glances
To slow down her steady advancing.
You'll need some pep pills to keep up with her,
'Cause Granny is learning break dancing.

She isn't content with her thoughts of old times;
Now she's always thirsting for knowledge.
So, don't bring your mending for Grandma to do
For Grandma has gone back to college.

If anyone's thinking of mugging our Gran
He'd better take heed of this warning;
She's learned how to toss a large man to the ground
From classes she goes to each morning.

If you want her to baby sit don't ring just yet -
She is bound to be back fairly soon.
She's floating above us a thousand feet up,
Riding high in a huge gas balloon.

So, don't bring her knitting - she's knitting her brow
Over holiday brochures to Spain.
And the glasses she uses are glasses of wine,
For she's off on her travels again.

Patsy Garner

THE SMALL MIRACLE

Father Frank was taking his daily walk
Before having his midday meal,
When he was approached by a stranger,
Dishevelled and quite down at heel;
This man of the road bluntly stated
'Twas a long time since he was last fed,
Then he asked for a little assistance
To help him buy his daily bread.

Father Frank was a shining example
Of real Christian charity,
Well known for his caring compassion
And his great generosity;
But he knew he was carrying no money,
He'd given all his spare cash away,
So sadly he turned to the other
And told him, 'There's nothing today.'

To prove that his statement was genuine,
His pockets he then turned out,
The second man watched him with interest,
On his face a faint shadow of doubt;
To the good Father's utter amazement,
A fifty-pence piece fell to earth,
The tramp then swooped swiftly upon it
And scampered for all he was worth.

Father Frank could hardly contain himself
And hurried back home to relate
The incident to his superior,
Whose reaction he then did await;
Said the older man, 'Miracles happen,
Like water being changed into wine,
But in future, please wear your own trousers
And don't leave the house wearing mine.'

Edward Farren

LITTLE SCAB

O little scab upon my knee
How I wonder much of thee
Like some band-aid, you're about
Stopping blood from leaking out

Methinks that thou art all congealed
Until my graze has fully healed
I cannot wait that long to find
You've left me with a scar behind

So as not to hurt my knee
I'll pluck thee off as quick can be
Then pop you in my mouth and chew
And so I shall recycle you.

Calvin Clarke

Such Is Life

My best friend was getting wed to a man I'd never met
He was wealthy, he was 'posh' but she told me not to fret
She'd told him lovely things about me; she said he'd love me too
And so the wedding came around and I knew what to do
I'm naturally an extrovert but I'd be prim and proper
My best intentions went to pot and I came such a cropper
I sank the sherries and the gins to toast the bride and groom
I went to sit down on a form to stop the spinning room
But I slipped down behind the bench and landed on my back
With my legs stuck up into the air - I really have the knack
The wedding cake upon my plate had disappeared from view
When I was helped upon my feet my consternation grew
In a loud and raucous voice I asked who'd pinched my wedding cake
I knew when I had uttered this it was a big mistake
I turned around to look for it and there was mass hysteria
The cake was firmly stuck upon my very large posterior
Could things get worse, I asked myself, for I felt such a clown
The look of horror on her face – I had let my best friend down
I was carried to the groom's Rolls Royce, we weren't going far
I shut his finger in the door and was sick in his new car
It took three of them to carry me and place me on my bed
I felt so very traumatised, I wished that I was dead
Next day they called with flowers and laughed till they did cry
Next time I get an invite I think I'll pass it by!

Rose Horscroft

The Meeting

The doggies held a meeting
They came from near and far
Some came by special aeroplane
Some came by motor car.

As they went into the meeting
Each was given a little book
And each one took his a******e off
And hung it on a hook.

When the meeting was going well
As sudden as was not
Came the strident clanging of the fire bell
And up the doggies shot.

They ran about in turmoil
They didn't stop to look
They just grabbed the nearest a******e
That was hanging on a hook.

So when you see a doggie sniffing another's bot
Don't be surprised because
As likely as is not
He's just checking if it's his, the other dog has got!

Roger Stevens

TICKETS PLEASE

I just arrived at Heaven
and knocked upon the door
it was opened by a lady
who I thought I'd seen before.

She looked me up and down
saying, 'This is not your door,
I think I met you down
below once or twice before.

Please let me see your ticket
have you just got off that cloud?'
I said, 'I really do not know
and my ticket is in my shroud.'

'There are no pockets in a shroud
how can that be so?
If you have not got your ticket
you will have to go below.'

Then I knew where I had met her
when we were down below,
a traffic warden in our town,
they called her Little Mo.

I thought we left that all behind
parking fines and so,
now she is up here on the gate
but now it's Mighty Mo.

Then a voice said, 'You are
dreaming, drink this cup of tea.'
With open eyes to my surprise
my darling wife I see.

James Hinder

CANDY

When I was just a teenager
We had a dog called Candy.
Her fur was coarse and scrubby
And her legs were rather bandy!

Her tail was proud and jaunty,
Her tummy barrel-round
(Because her legs were very short
It nearly touched the ground!)

She loved her tit-bits - chocolate drops
Were Candy's favourite treat.
She'd nose in people's pockets
Just to see what she could eat.

Her ears were sharp, her hearing was
'Selective' shall we say -
She could hear a toffee wrapper
From half a mile away!

I made a raincoat (just for fun -
Cut from a plastic mac)
It had a hood and four short legs
With a tail-hole at the back!

The sight of Candy in her coat
Made people stare and stop.
She caused a fair commotion
Tied outside the butchers' shop!

She bore it all with dogged air,
Head high for all to see -
A stoic little dachshund
With a lot of dignity!

Rosemary Williams

NIGHTMARING

'I've swallowed the budgerigar
Help me to stand on my head
Before it goes down any further
I do hope the poor thing's not dead.'
How they laughed at my efforts
To regurgitate. I could hardly speak
I alone was aware that the lump going down
Was the family pet's sharp beak.
To give them their due they searched
And I helped without a word
My heart wasn't in it
For only I knew for certain
Where was the bird.
We had been speaking as usual
Words of endearment
In the kitchen while washing up
Joey on top of his cage leant
To far towards my open mouth
Down, down my throat he went.
I wasn't surprised no one believed me
I could hardly believe it myself
Except in the night when I wake with a tweak
In my stomach and reach to the shelf
For anti-acid - then I remember the beak
And go back to sleep.
Hoping this time to dream
A little less realistically
While Joey gives an occasional peep
From his perch in the kitchen
Safely asleep.

Betty Gilman

ANTIQUES ROGUESHOW

Genuine punters beware
I'm not an antique armchair,
I've been valued high
So experts who buy
Will have a few quid going spare.

Knackered in all departments
Sagged where I ought to be plump,
My webbing is slack
There's no turning back -
My bottom could drop with a thump.

Legs are shapely but wobble
Seating collapsed in despair,
Just sit on my throw
Your rear end will know
Whose springs are in need of repair.

When disillusioned woodworm
Select a suicide spray,
We fill in their tracks
Then polish with wax -
The experts are fooled every day.

Doreen Lovey

To Build, Or Not To Build?

There once was a builder called Jack
Who had trouble constructing a shack
The shape of the roof
Was final proof
That really he hadn't the knack

When requested to fit a new tank in a loft
He drew on a fag, 'Is the water hard or soft?'
And needed to know
For the rooms below
'It'll determine the damage,' he coughed

He hired a cement mixer and made up a mix
Then Jack found the job was just too big to fix
He forgot the cement
And now we lament
It set solid and the hirer knocked him for six

When called out to unblock a big drain
'Is it sewage?' he asked, 'Or water from the rain?'
There was no reply
He looked at the sky
And decided he could not stand the strain

Jack's skills were forever put to the test
And of course, as always, he did his best
But, as they say
There comes the day
When it's safer to put your feet up and rest.

Derek Harvey

CLOVER

(A much missed friend)

He brought such happy moments,
He always made us smile,
He did such naughty, cheeky things,
We had him for a while.
We closed the doors, we hid the fruit,
We moved and blocked so much,
We preferred he was indoors with us,
Than stuck out in his hutch.
He chewed our books, removed the webs
Of dust around our home,
Upon our laps he'd bring to us
Stripped wire from the phone.
He brought us notes and gnawed our shoes,
Collapsed upon our feet,
He was the funniest character
You could ever wish to meet.
His ears they flopped, his face was bent,
His teeth were not much good,
We had them trimmed, he did behave,
Once short, he'd eat his food.
He had a chum, his elephant,
All pink and grey was she,
He held her close and cuddled her
For everyone to see.
We shan't forget that special bun,
As long as there's still fate.
He loved us all, we loved him too,
Old Clover, our true mate!

Geraldine Frances Sanders

The Pants

As I was walking home from work one dark, cold, breezy night
I heard a strange pinging sound, it gave me quite a fright.
I carried on walking, feeling a little uneasy,
My bum felt quite cold, the wind was very breezy.
As I carried on walking, I discovered something odd,
The pinging sound was the broken elastic from my pants, I am a poor old sod.
I struggled home quickly as my pants were nearly coming down
And when I told my family, they laughed just like a lot of clowns.
Those pants have really had it, they ain't no good for me,
It's clear they are worn out and have lost their elasticity.
They belong in the bin and that's where they're gonna go,
The pants are so embarrassing, they have really caused me stress,
I really want some proper pants, not ones with loose elastic that end up in a mess.
I want a brand new pair that I can safely wear,
Ones that keep my bum all nice and cosy,
'Cause your ass should be warm, not cold and rosy.
I hope this cheeky tale will put a smile on everyone's face
And send out lots of laughter all over the place.

Toni Attew

TOPSY-TURVY WORLD

I live in a topsy-turvy world
Where I sleep under my bed.
My slippers, I wear backwards
And my tights wrapped around my head.

My front door's round the back,
The windows are on the floor,
The carpet I had fit on the ceiling,
The neighbours really can't take anymore.

I live in a topsy-turvy world,
With a dustbin lid as my bath.
I keep all good books, like everyone should,
In my shed just by the back path.

My clothes I keep in the kitchen
And the veggies in the front room.
My car is parked on next door's roof
And I comb my hair with the broom.

I live in a topsy-turvy world
Where everything's upside down.
I walk on my head and when I sleep under my bed,
I dream of the world the right way around.

Gillian Clarke

Grow Up!

Poor boy sitting still
Rich boy playing so
Poor man sitting still
Rich man playing so
Men never grow up!

Simon Ward

A Cry From The Heart

What a stupid place to put it,
Halfway up the door;
You cannot even reach it
Unless you walk across the floor.

I can simply not believe
When a room is long and thin,
That anyone would put it there,
On the door where you come in.

Perhaps I could throw something
And with luck I'd knock it down,
But then if someone hears me,
I'll be the laughing stock of town.

But after all, I am a guest,
I can't stay here all day;
I just don't know what to do,
Whatever will people say.

You feel absolutely helpless,
As if stuck down with glue,
When the toilet paper's out of reach
And you're sitting on the loo.

Robert Quin

OUR SUE

Sue was two
And didn't talk
I was five and did
Our Sue sat
In her high chair
With mashed up food and wearing a bib

Mum stood up
And left the room
'Behave yourselves,' she said
When she'd gone
I took the lunch
And tipped it on Sue's head

Food ran down her baby cheeks
And stuck inside her hair
Sue cried out and Mum rushed in
And pulled her from her chair

I just sat there
As good as gold
While Sue took all the blame
I was five
But now I feel so ashamed.

David Sheasby

The Terrorist Twos

The red wellies that you loved before,
Today you simply hate.
You've thrown your juice onto the floor,
Again once more we're late!

Your chubby fist fastens on the cat
Poor Kitty loudly squawks.
I rescue her - then discover that
You're in her litter-box!

I haul you out and fetch a brush
Now my eyes meet such a scene,
White-crested waves towards me rush,
You've opened the washing machine!

Remind me please, whose idea was it
Being a mother'd be a breeze?
We have to rush - I'm just not fit -
Don't microwave Mummy's keys!

007 - that macho spy,
The KGB could not annoy him,
Let the truth be told 'twixt you and I
My little darling would destroy him!

I shoulder open the car door
And try to strap you in,
You stiffen out and start to roar
Your head butts me on the chin.

Across my cheek your little nails rake
Now you're going wild,
You're almost three, for Heaven's sake,
Stop acting like a child!

Maureen Dawson

THRONE

I sat upon the throne
A book was in my hand,
I thought quite pleasantly
That this was mighty grand

Peace and quiet did I have
No one to bother me,
With nothing to distract
At least that I could see.

When all was finished
Arise I tried to go,
But there was no paper
To wipe, yes! You know.

I looked around
In despair
Nothing I could see,
For there was nil
I could use
To try and clean me.

My precious book
I had to use
Oh what a waste,
I reckon that poor author
Would think it in bad taste.

The moral of the story is
Make sure that you can see
Plenty of paper all around
To clean what you *can't* see.

Jack Lanigan

Little Willie

Little Willie put a leech
Down Paul's pants and made him screech.
Paul went to tell the teacher,
She put Willie through the mincer!

Matthew Pye (10)

Little Willie

Little Willie growing thinner
Shot a rabbit for his dinner
Sadly, realised too late
Next door's pussy filled his plate

Little Willie knew not how
The simple way to milk a cow
His tugging efforts, so extreme
Filled the pail with clotted cream

Little Willie thought he'd try
To bake a tasty apple pie
When he tripped and took a tumble
He landed in an apple crumble

Footballer Willie played the game
His married life, not quite the same
Resulting every Saturday
One wife at home and one away.

Eveline Weighell

My Advertising Hell

Through my letterbox they all pour,
Promising fortune, cars, holidays and so much more.
Why not invest, insure, have this credit card?
Catalogues that are full of things that you'll never need,
I even get adverts telling me what I should read.

Buy any magazine it will contain more blurb than you know,
I keep on saying to one in particular, no, no, no.
Just leave me alone to get on with my life
Without all this wasted paper, scratch cards, causing only strife.

The chance of any of us being left alone is very dim,
So I'm just gonna have to keep on filling up my wheelie bin.

Susan Barker

ODE TO FLU

Lock me in a padded cell,
Where it's warm and clean.
Just give me a box of tissues
And a nice warm jet of steam.

My eyes they're all watery,
My nose, it's gone all red,
I haven't got the energy
To leave this ruddy bed.

My body is all shaky,
My cheeks are totally pale,
My tongue is like a boulder
In a mouth that is so stale.

Don't hug me or kiss me,
I'm all full of germs,
The sweat is just pouring,
My body, one big ache.
This flu is one problem
I can't seem to shake.

When will this be over?
Not for a week or two!
Someone get the doctor
So I can feel as good as new.

Next time I'm gonna be prepared,
Hot water bottles and the like,
I don't want to feel like this again
On these long, cold winter nights.

Donna Salisbury

LITTLE HELPER

Ummm, which shall I have?
I'm always hungry after a nap,
Bic-bics, bic-bics fill the gap.
Orr-orr, look at those crumbs I've made,
But Grandma likes to be my slave.
I find the brush and dustpan
And she takes it from my hand,
I like to push the big brush,
But somehow the plants' leaves fall off
And Grandma isn't pleased.
The dick-dicks don't like it when I leave.

I often get stuck-stuck
And they always rush to see,
It usually makes them grin
At the predicament I'm in.
'Mind the step,' is Grandma's favourite saying,
She's frightened she'll find me there laying.
Whenever it is quiet,
She finds me in a trice,
I like to tidy her bedside drawer
But she insists I 'play' a bit more.

The television and radio need tuning in,
The clicking of the buttons is fascinating
And they never have it hot enough,
No wonder I get a cough,
But Grandma's little helper
Doesn't even get a day off.

Sylvia Shafto

At The Pictures

When I was a girl of precisely six,
My mother took me to the flicks.
The Sound Of Music would be a treat
With plenty of songs and popcorn to eat.
There were Julie Andrews, children and nuns –
I didn't take in the German guns.

Now my father had left my mother and me
In the care of an extended family.
My grandmother was loving, but with a Victorian bent
For being grateful for every good thing that was sent.

At that age, I didn't follow what was going on -
My ears pricked up at the start of a song;
So I didn't realise the Baron's children weren't blessed
With a mother, as she'd been laid to rest.
But for some reason I still don't know to this day,
I happened to catch the Baron say

To his children, 'You're going to have a new mother.'
Well! I went all hot under the collar!
'Having two mummies!' I blurted out in a flurry,
'I'm lucky enough to have one mummy!'

Kathy Rawstron

TALKING SHOE

I heard a funny noise from my wardrobe did come,
Little did I know my shoes were having fun.
I peeped inside and what did I see?
Shoes a-giggling and dancing free.
'She'll pick me up,' the Gold said to the Brown,
'We're going out and it's not to town.'
'I don't know about that,' said the weary boot,
'It's cold out there, it's me she'll choose.'
'Give it a rest, Boot, she always chooses you,
It's because you're old and worn through.'
'Please yourself,' said Boot with a sigh,
'I'm not like you, delicate and high.'
The sandal was far, far from amused,
It could not come up with any excuse.
'I'll wait for warm weather,' she said rather cross.
'Be quiet,' said Slipper, 'good sleep I have lost.'
All of a sudden the door opened wide
And out came shoe with splits on the side.
'Well, that's that,' said Brown, 'sales are on the book
And there's one thing you've overlooked.
You may not be here next week, but in a charity shop,
With new owner who doesn't have a lot.'

Carol Boneham

I Never Ever Knew

I carried home a parcel for a lady late one night
From Shepherds Bush to Bayswater -
I thought that I did right.
But to my grief, at Holland Park
The package split in twain
And out did fall a tiny bag -
It filled my heart with pain.
To see that small thing lying there
All crumpled in the snow,
Whatever then to say to her
I really did not know.

For in that bag were gold-brown crisps -
Her supper, that's for sure
And as I think about it now
I worry even more.
I worry what she thinks of me
And what I should have said
And worry, did she have some food
Before she went to bed?

Kenneth Kirby

THE RIGHT ADJECTIVE

Mum, I've lost the bloody ball
In those bloody nettles there.
Oh Johnny, you must not say that.
There's no blood on them anywhere.
'Bloody' means there's blood on it,
Just like when you cut your knee.
The ball is yellow, nettles green,
You really must speak properly.

We'll take a walk around the field,
It's such a lovely, spring-like day.
The birds are nesting in the hedge,
We'll watch the newborn lambs at play.
Barbed wire! Now you go underneath,
I'll hold it. Watch your little head.
Now I'll climb over. Oh! I'm caught.
'You've cut your bloody leg,' John said.

Elizabeth Millington

THE OFFICER

There once was a fellow named Willoughby-Gore,
Whose nickname's 'Gore-Blimey,' and that is for sure.
Now, he was an officer, though he's a clot;
But not in the Navy, for which thanks a lot!

He was not in the Air Force; d'you want to know why?
The reason is simple: this chap couldn't fly.
And neither was he in the Army, to boot;
Once again it's quite simple: this chap couldn't shoot.

He was not in the Navy, nor Air Force, nor Army,
But he's still an officer, so someone's barmy.
He was put in charge of a large group of men
Who gave him his 'Gore-Blimey' nickname right then.

He was put in charge of a firing squad,
Or a Fire Brigade station, till one day - oh, God:
He started to panic, with results that were dire -
So his men hosed him down every time he yelled, 'Fire!'

Roger Williams

UNTITLED

Rafferty's pig was a wonderful animal,
Built like a battleship, solid and stout,
Ignorance fit to disgrace any cannibal,
Impudence written all over its snout.

The night it broke loose it caused such a commotion,
Women were screaming and men turning pale.
Running and jumping, colliding and bumping
With everyone making a grab at its tail.

Mickey Malone, the town's heavyweight champion,
Rushed at the pig with a big rolling pin,
Struck it a blow that hit Molly Monroe
And doubled her bustle right under her chin!

Molly Monroe, she fell through a shop window,
In eggs and tomatoes and pickles she lay,
Eggs and 'tomayters; all over her gaiters,
The night that the pig ran away.

R Vincent

Quality Time

I was having a coffee in the corner café,
When a strange little man came up to me.
He was all dressed up in see-through cling film,
His cap and boots were banana skins.
He had come-to-bed eyes, a lop-sided grin
And a gap in his teeth like the Grand Canyon.

I was measuring the floor
From my chair to the door,
Ready to make an emergency escape,
When he burst into song,
'Come along, come along,
How would you like to
Spend some quality time with me?
You will see the world through different eyes,
Because I live up a tree.

You could share my nest in the sycamore tree,
With the moon and stars for company.
You would be as safe as houses
With a man like me.
Do you want to hear my battle cry?'
He thumped his chest and let out a yell,
The management told him, 'Go to Hell!'
'Come along sister, don't be shy,
I'm begging you, please give it a try.
Spend some quality time with me,
Don't miss a golden opportunity.'

I drained the last drop from my coffee cup,
Undecided, I looked up. I was all alone,
The how-would-you-like-to-man was gone,
Leaving me with some quality time.

Beth Izatt Anderson

Little Willie

Little Willie always cross
Thought he was the very boss,
Always shouting at the boys
For making such a lot of noise.

People never shout at him
'Cause they knew they'd be int bin,
Little Willie, such a bully,
Always throwing kids int gully.

Laura Wilson (9)

LITTLE WILLIE

Little Willie what a Billy
Climbed a wall and had a fall.
He broke his leg and hit his head
So Mother sent him off to bed.

Emma Pinder (10)

LITTLE WILLIE

Little Willie wasn't good,
Didn't do what he should,
Never listened in his class,
Always broke the window glass.

Little Willie trashed the house,
Then he killed a little mouse,
His mother sent him up to bed,
On the way he bumped his head.

Kirsty Swarbrick (10)

DEAREST DUSTMEN

Dearest Dustmen, how's your bins now?
We have washed out all our tins now
Glass and sharp things wrapped up tightly
All hot ashes, cooled over nightly.
Weeds and cuttings put for compost
Paper wrappings in the bin tossed
Old newspapers sent for mashing
Your new lorry's really smashing
Your young gang too, all shave daily
Like to meet them at a ceilidh
So keep smiling Hampshire bin men
We all love you, fat and thin men
Drive your Vulture oh, so gently
Make it sound like a new Bentley.

Denis M Pentlow

THE FUNNY SIDE OF LIFE

A young man went to the doctor,
He was not feeling quite himself,
But the doctor was getting a bit fed up,
For this visit was now his twelfth.
'I know full well I'm a donkey,'
Is what the young man said,
'For although I've got a human body,
I've got a donkey's head.'
The doctor looked him in the eye,
There was nothing wrong, of course.
'Last week you had the head of a dog,
The week before it was a horse,
You've turned into so many animals,
You're almost a complete zoo,
So take yourself down to the local beach
And join the donkey queue
And before you give the kids a ride,
Take off your rose-tinted glasses,
Then note the difference between yourself
And all the other asses.
And when you've given the kids a ride,
You'll find yourself in pain
And then when you return to human form,
Come back and see me again.'

Joan Gilchrist

Kept His Eye On The Ball

It was at the junior football match,
A father, a high-kicked ball, he tried to catch.
Step by step backward, eyes on said ball,
Without looking behind, into the net he did fall.

Firmly entangled like a hapless fish,
'Earth open up and swallow me,' was his wish,
From conspiring silence to hearty laughter aloud,
He became the main attraction of the crowd.

Too stunned to speak or laugh,
He was asked, 'Why are you eating your scarf?'
Still bound tight, embarrassed and smeared with dirt,
He managed to mutter, 'My landing gear's hurt.'

After helping hands pulled him away,
Through pained expression, 'Thanks,' was all he could say,
Then from the mouth of a babe named Rob,
'Goalkeeper? Don't' give up your day job.'

Brett Lovett

BAH, HUMBUG!

You know it's nearly Christmas
When you visit BHS -
They've glitter, baubles, tacky gifts,
It looks a bloomin' mess.

The card shops get their cards in
Even though it's just September,
But if you buy them you won't find them
When you need them in December.

Your mother starts to wind you up
She really drives you mad
And when she burns the Christmas cakes
She blames it on poor Dad.

The house must all be tidy,
Cos the relatives are invited
And when they hand you tacky gifts
You have to look delighted.

(When Aunt Joan hands her gift to me
I think I'll have to thump her
If her present, just like every year
Is another home-made jumper!)

I don't know why we celebrate
Each Christmas the same way -
Mum says that it's tradition
But I'd call it Groundhog Day.

The sprouts are always soggy
When we have our Christmas dinner
And grandma always says to Mum,
'That turkey was a winner!'

We never manage pudding
(Which is good, cos I'm not keen,)
Then Dad and Grandad fall asleep
While we all watch the Queen.

But the one good thing at Christmas
And it cannot go unsaid,
Is that there's no school for two whole weeks
So I get to lie in bed!

Tracey Kay Dean

COULDNA' WAIT

Oh dearie me,
I'm needin' a pee
A couldna' get there quicker
So a dun it in ma knickers
The door wiz locked, a had nae key
I've got a wet patch, look n' see.

Oh dearie me,
I'm burstin' for a pee
I tried ta tell ya, I couldna wait
Now A'm tellin' you, it's too late
Have another look n' see
It's already 'it ma knee.

Oh dearie me,
Am desperate for a pee
You said a couldna go the noo
We'd have tae try n' find a loo
It disna bother me nae mare
See the puddle on the flare
Oh dearie me,
A dinnae need a pee.

Dale Finlay

LEGENDARY

He's a legend in his own mind,
Mixing freely with his own kind,
Mouth always open, it won't close,
Like Pinocchio he's got a big nose.

He answers questions before you can ask,
Getting on your case, his life's task,
Conversations, to which he's not invited,
He butts in, thinking he's been slighted.

If in a debate he was on your side,
His knowledge then would be sorely tried,
He's like no one person you've ever known,
Just like a child, in a world of his own.

He's a know all, a mind like a steel trap,
His voice drones on and on, yappity yap,
He still mixes freely with his own kind,
But still he's a legend *in his own mind.*

Nicholas Maughan

Aphrodite

Here lies the body of Patrick
Meredith Golightly
Who, even when he was geriatric,
Lifted a nightie excitedly.
He tried too hard for the hat trick
Night after nightly;
He thought he was tough as a house brick
And very sprightly -
His death was quick and dramatric
And quite rightly.

Tony MacMillan

WHAT MADE GREAT BRITAIN GREAT

What made Great Britain great, I swear,
What gave us confidence and flair,
What made we Brits so debonair,
Was Marks and Spencer's underwear.

From royalty to pauper's heir,
From humble man to millionaire,
They wore next to their bottoms bare,
Their Marks and Spencer's underwear.

From tiny tots, without a care,
To grandma in her rocking chair,
Each comforted their derriere
With Marks and Spencer's underwear.

We all had one pair - and a spare
At least, or there was great despair!
We were content, none could compare
With Marks and Spencer's underwear.

What made Great Britain great, was their
Exclusive nether region wear.
And worn by all - oh who would dare
Mock Marks and Spencer's underwear?

Jax Burgess

The Red Indian

The Red Indian sat cross-legged in his tent,
His thoughts to meditate were heaven-sent.
He waited for the answers from on high
From the Great White Spirit in the sky.

His visualisations were very clear,
But words that were said, he could not hear.

He listened again, but all in vain,
The images were clear, but the words never came.

Then his vision showed why he heard no sound,
While meditating, cross-legged on the ground.

After being shown, he let out a cheer,
Now seeing the reason why, so clear.

His bewilderment gone now, he had no fear,
His hearing aid had fallen into his beer.

Jemma James

The Snowball Fight

I joined the winning side, I thought,
They had the best supplies -
Across the snow-filled fields we trudged,
The opposition spied.

I filled my scarf with snow 'bombs,'
The enemy in sight,
Then Billy shouted *fire,*
And so began the fight.

We held our line with courage,
Though outnumbered we fought on -
As ice froze to my fingers,
I was lost among the throng.

With a childish whoop of victory,
Another strike was won -
My comrades cheered and shook my hand
For the fine job I had done.

Alas, I had to leave my friends
For 'I can't be late for tea!'
Dripping wet, but glowing,
Oh, what a fuss there'll be!

As I stand here grinning sheepishly
In the puddle by the door,
'Snow bombs!' she yells, 'I ask you!
You're a man of sixty-four!'

Jill Darroch

DECISIONS, DECISIONS!

I would have, I should have, but I didn't.
Decisions, decisions.
Is it Plan A or is it Plan B?
I just can't decide,
I'll toss a coin.
Heads for Plan A, tails for Plan B,
But I don't care for either,
So I'll go for Plan C.
The decision is to make no decision,
Just wait and see.
Hindsight, they tell me, is a wonderful thing,
So I'll sit back and watch the birdies sing.

Henry Rayner

A Sad Loss

The gale that made the grey spume fly
Made rags of clouds up in the sky,
Sundered you and I forever,
Though I'd thought you'd leave me never.

I can't forget that fateful day,
How silently you slipped away,
There was no warning, no goodbye,
I heard no last departing sigh.

I held you close, folk smiled to see
The way I kept you close to me,
A hair's breadth and it was no more,
Between us as we strolled that shore.

Oh, who could know, that fateful day,
So suddenly you'd fly away;
Though by a power underpinned,
We are but chaff upon the wind.

It is a source of pain to me,
Your empty place, which now I see:
The third drawer down, beneath the phone,
A little nest I made your own.

And now it's June, how time does fly,
It seems the months just whistle by,
Who now remembers that bleak day,
The day my hat was snatched away!

S Mainwaring

MUMMY'S ASHES

There were two sisters
At a convent guest house.
They brought with them
A small wooden box,
Carrying it around in turn,
And in the dining room
Placing it carefully on the table.

It looked like a musical box
Or something similar,
But it did transpire
That it was a casket,
Containing Mummy's ashes
Which she'd wished scattered
In the convent grounds.

With some ceremony
They chose the spot,
Accompanied by a Sister,
But the box would not open.
Sister hurried to the convent
A screwdriver to obtain.

Then disaster struck -
Facing *into* the wind,
Mummy's ashes were scattered
Over Sister's gown and veil!
Returning to the guest house
She shook off Mummy's ashes
On to the guest house floor!

Poor Mummy! An undignified end.
Her ashes were hoovered up.
But what could we do?
I hope, wherever Mummy is,
That she will understand
With, perhaps, a rueful smile!

Maria-Christina

LITTLE WILLIE

Little Willie, what a pain,
Always messing with teacher's cane.
Oh Willie, please make a Christmas card,
He slapped his teacher very hard.

Little Willie got put in the bin,
His head got stuck in a tin.

Sarah Rhodes (11)

LITTLE WILLIE POEMS

Little Willie was in a mood
He saw the teacher dancing nude,
She never saw him stand and stare
And now he's in intensive care.

Little Willie ate the fish
Then licked up the cat's dish.
He made such a mess on the kitchen floor,
Then his mother slammed his head in the door.

Little Willie had a car
Then covered it up with black horrid tar.
The cat sat on it and got such a fright,
When he came home, Willie set it alight.

Little Willie went to school,
Called the tiny ones little fools.
The teacher saw him and took him to the head,
So she got out a gun and shot him dead.

Little Willie was a brat,
Called the teacher very fat.
She pulled him up by his hair
And made in walk in his underwear.

Bryony Greenway (9)

LITTLE WILLIE

Little Willie in a mood
Told his teacher something rude,
The teacher kicked him on the shin,
Shoved him head first in the bin.

Laura Fisher (10)

TILL KETTLE STOPS!

The kettle's on
and anyway, in days bygone -
my Gramp and Granny wouldn't dare to stare
at you or even say, 'Hi there!' in church
(that fusty word) one that, in the 20s was not heard
to be the thing
now known to bring
comfort and love and oh, such glee!
It was said to be
The dreaded words, 'Lord' and 'Church', words which brought
into a web of fear, caught right up amidst the year's
fights and tussles, bangs and bombs, all loss -
yet now I've time to offer thought
I really have to your feet brought
all of that shrapnel, hate and so, Lord, (if poss)
when this kettle's boiled,
would you blot out all those bits I've soiled
and in my few years without *you,* I come and offer
all that *you* have done - around the world with banner unfurled -
along with the cross and from now on, yes,
You're my boss!

Jac C Simmons

Chuck Them Out

Happy Christmas!
New Year!
Season's greetings all!
It's time for jokes and gaiety
And gifts and cakes and fun -
And sprouts!
Brussels sprouts!
Small cannon balls of concentrated cabbage on my plate -
Which I hate!
Please, give me a Christmas without the sprouts.
I'll say it again to leave you in no doubt . . .
I want a Christmas without the sprouts!

The build up is great.
The presents a treat.
The baubles
The lights
The crackers
The sweets
But the sprouts?
Chuck them out!
I'm sure the fun of cakes and gifts
The gaiety of jokes
And all the greetings of the season,
A year new past its post,
Would be best if the roast
Had no sprouts.
Chuck them out!

Colin Hogan

OVERRUN

The trouble with some folks,
They never stop talking,
Every subject under the sun,
From flea pits to bottled perfumery!
Why doesn't someone zip her up?
Lockwood? Berry-Brow? Honley? Brockholes?
I should have left the train at Honley
To give a talk to the 'Women's Bright Hour'!
I can just see their expression register,
'Never have we been so late before,
What shall we do?' Poor you!
I'll have a drink at the nearest pub
And write a poem entitled,
'Never Converse With Strange Women.'
That woman's never-resting tongue
Would take me to Land's End!
The perfect dropping off spot!

Mary Dearnley

SEEING DOUBLE

I've tried to buy trousers to fit my large rear,
But always some problem comes up, I fear.
Too long, too short, too tight, what a figure
And not only that . . . it seems to get bigger!
Metric measurements fox me. I can't sort them out.
Can't we go back to inches? For me they've more clout.
I'm too fond of the sweet things, that's my trouble,
I'll have to cut down, then my waistline won't double.
In the meantime, my slacks are anything but!
Oh, calamity! Where have I put my left foot?

E Balmain

Little Willie And His Habits

Little Willie is a brat
Always hitting people with a bat,
Putting glue on teacher's chair
And ending up all in her hair,
So he was made to sit on the mat,
Like I said, he is a brat.

Linzi Graves (9)

Wit v Whoops!

It's odd that what makes some folk laugh
Won't even make me smile
And how they stare, bemused and grave
When I'm rolling in the aisle.

It's funny how banana skins
Became a laughing symbol;
It's jolly painful - as I know
For I'm not all that nimble.

But repartee is something else.
I relish every quip,
I roll it round my tongue and grin.
So here's a handy tip . . .

The next time that you see me smile
In a vacant sort of way,
Remember that for some of us
There's pleasure in word-play.

D M Anderson

Little Willie

Little Willie was a silly Billy
He chased young girls all round the privy.
When Teacher did come there
He put a hacksaw through her chair.

Little Willie was an oaf and a bully,
Would cheat other kids out of their dinner money.
Little Willie was caught
And with a group of kids he fought.
When Teacher arrived there,
There's a lesson to be taught here somewhere.

Raymond Law

SLOW SLED TO MADEIRA

We'd heard a lot of the thrilling ride
On the downhill slope in Madeira,
Of hurtling speeds and thrills wide-eyed
As zero hour drew nearer.
We viewed the scene from a waiting queue,
An ancient and glamorous attraction,
We watched the sleds go screaming down,
With visions of James Bond in action.
The men in control were an awesome sight,
Manly and bronzed and so young,
All of them dressed in immaculate white,
Strapping in sinew and lung.
Our turn came at last to plunge down the slope,
Nerves stirring and minds full of tension,
The men on each side didn't radiate hope,
Must've been drawing their pension.
As the sled gently stumbled its leisurely way
Came a noise like the jarring of points,
It wasn't the sound of a fast moving sleigh,
But of ancient and arthritic joints.
All the other sleds passed us at nerve-racking pace
As we ground to a stop on some high land,
The two who had guided our tortoise-like race
Were the oldest two men on the island.
It offered the chance of just one more run,
We'd issue a quick, harsh decliner,
In fact we're quite sure we'd have much more fun
If we took a slow boat to China!

Jack Scrafton

LITTLE WILLIE POEMS

Little Willie thumped his teacher,
Stood up on a box to reach her,
In return she used her cane,
He won't be doing that again.

Little Willie, round the houses,
Saw a girl and dropped his trousers,
She dragged him home and told his mum,
Who kicked him smartly up his bum.

Little Willie dialled '999',
Spun the fire brigade a line,
Police came round to Willie's place,
Said hoax calls cause a lot of waste.

Little Willie went to t' shops
And nicked some sweets, they called the cops,
They took him home and his mum did tell,
She banged him round the head as well!

Mick Nash

Little Willie's Day

Little Willie found a rat,
Put it in his grandpa's hat,
Should've heard our Willie scream,
The hat was his, twas just a dream.

Little Willie spilt the milk,
Blamed his brother, smooth as silk,
When his brother didn't cry,
Willie poked him in the eye.

Little Willie bold as brass,
Bullied his sister - poor wee lass,
When she said, 'I'm telling Mum,'
Willie kicked her on the bum.

Little Willie wouldn't bath,
He told his mother with a laugh,
Mother said, 'Now don't be silly,
You can't be a dirty Willie.'

Little Willie bad deeds all done,
Went to bed at ten to one,
Planning and plotting all the while,
Little Willie fell asleep with a smile.

S M Hooper

WILLIE'S PET WHITE MOUSE

Little Willie's mum got a fright
When she got up for a wee in the night
Willie bought a friend for his pet mouse
They've now infested the whole blooming house!

John Worthington

Little Willie

Little Willie was not wise
He told an awful lot of lies
His mother thought him such a dear
Although she often clipped his ear.

Little Willie made so much noise
He bashed up all the children's toys
Mother said, 'Well never mind,'
But Father kicked his little behind.

Little Willie one day, went too far
He squeezed the family kitten into a jar
Mother said, 'We've got another cat,'
But Father went to beat the little brat.

Joan Hammond

Little Willie The Vampire

Little Willie did enquire
Why friends called him vampire?
Mum said, 'Ignore those tiny tots
And drink your soup before it clots.'

Ray Ford

LITTLE WILLIE!

Little Willie, en route to school,
kicks at water in a pool,
splashes mud up Chloe's dress,
her face, her socks, a terrible mess!

Little Willie travels by car,
thinks it fun to shout at Ma,
when she runs into the gate,
she shouts, 'Stop it Willie, or we'll be late.'

Willie has picked a facial spot,
made it bleed - quite a lot,
needs a cloth to clear the mess,
decides to use Mama's new dress.

Little Willie, how we're not sure,
poked his legs through the attic door,
Mother, startled, remonstrates,
one brown, one blue sock don't look great.

Willie, in a fit of great duress
set fire to a waste basket, what a mess!
With Miss' best perfume Willie doused the flames,
then dashed to the playground to resume his games.

Little Willie has got no sense,
he tried to climb the garden fence,
he got half-way and then got stuck
and Mother said, 'Best read your book.'

Lynda Burton

AT SEVENTEEN (1942)

I thought that I'd become a nurse
Like my dear Auntie Lou
So off I went, a might averse
For my first interview,
Matron fixed me with stony glare,
I quivered in my shoes
'I wonder girl if you're aware
That this career you've chose
Is hard work like you've never known
And right for very few,
You're tall and strong, I like your tone
I think that you will do,
You'll move into the nurses home
With Russell and nurse Robb.
You'll get your keep and uniform
And two pounds a month for the job.'
Quarter past six our morning call
Quick swill under the tap
Then on down to the breakfast hall
Grab a clip to hold your cap.
Sister in charge of porridge and prunes
With half an hour to dine
Ward duty then till afternoon
Bed pan chores were mine.
Busy scrubbing down in the sluice
Singing in my best voice
Heard Matron calling, 'What the deuce?
Nurse will you stop that noise?'
I decided that this nursing lark
Was really not for me
I left and wed my sailor boy
And am happy as can be.

J Fletcher

KEEPING UP APPEARANCES

A simple walk there never is, when you are at my side,
We have to stop at park so you - 'can have another ride'.

You rush down slide, shout out loud, 'Nanny, you come do it too!'
And then 'again', 'again' and 'more'! Till I am all askew!

My hair is standing up on end, my glasses perched off nose.
My knickers showing at my waist, boobs droop for pop-out shows!

My skirt now riding up my thighs, my tights are riding down
I hope I don't meet those I know, when walking back through town.

Now I sit in wooden train - am taken to a zoo
But realise I am sitting in a pile of sticky goo!

Then it's rush to other end of park to grab a chance . . .
to sit astride a plastic horse and gallop off to France!

The horse is wet and so am I, my scarf has dropped in mud
Lean down, retrieve, then overbalance, land in a puddle, *thud!*

Now looking like the rag man, I hear? Oh no! Four clicks!
Your mum has got her camera out and taken more sick pics!

Di Castle

THE MAYPOLE

Once again it was May Day
The music played
The boys and girls
Picked up their ribbons
Ready to dance round
The Maypole.
Round and round
Under and over
Not even getting tangled up
Making a lovely splash of colour
Then all of a sudden
Kathleen shrieked,
'My elastic's gone on my knickers,'
Elizabeth said, 'Keep dancing,'
And pushed her forward
Hoping she would step out of her knickers.
To her horror
Everyone went bashing into one another
After that episode
She has never been seen since.

E Bevans

THE UNIVERSITY OF LIFE

I worked in a hotel to make a living,
For customer service I was always giving.
A few moments of laughter I'll share with you
And can help cheer up a day which may seem blue.

I noticed a man looking about,
'Can I help you,' I did shout.
He replied, 'I hope you can my son,
They say, *dogs are to be carried on lift and I cannot find one.*'

Another time I was helping out,
On porter duty while heart and back held stout.
Asking for a tip after struggling with bags up ten flights
The gentleman offered, 'Never mix your colours with your whites.'

A group of dog lovers descended our hotel,
Yapping mutts, peeing and poohing, making my life hell.
They held the sheepdog trials later that week,
Seven dogs found guilty of making the carpets reek.

In the hotel, staff and customers always shared a joke
And it showed me, 'there's nowt queerer than folk'.
But at the hotel I met my wife
And continue to study there at the University of Life.

Kenny McAlpine

SECOND THOUGHTS

I hate this family, I hate this house.
My sister's a pain, my brother's a louse.
He borrowed my bike without asking me,
I locked him in the shed and hid the key.

Though I whispered, 'Sorry,' I still got the blame.
It's so unfair - my life's pure pain.
'I'm leaving,' I screamed, to which my mum said,
'I'll make you sandwiches - white or brown bread?

I suppose,' she added, 'you've no time to shop?
I promised you new jeans; no doubt you forgot?'
Oh no! And that boat trip! Dad's birthday treat.
'I'm starving, Mum, is there something to eat?'

Margaret Gregory

IT'S HER FAVOURITE

I don't know what she'll do,
when that old jumper wears out.
She bought it in America,
it's her favourite, I've no doubt.
She wears it quite often,
well, nearly every day.
I quite believe it's something,
that she'll never throw away.
When she's not wearing it,
it's in the washing machine.
'Cos even though it's wearing thin,
she likes to keep it clean.
She has a wardrobe full of clothes,
that she don't care about.
So unless it's a special occasion,
she gets the jumper out.
She always makes sure she's looking good,
especially her hair.
But when it comes to clothes,
well let's just say, I know what she will wear.

Janet Eves

MY DOCTOR'S SURGERY

When I'm sick and feeling low
Down to the doctors I must go.

I give my name and take a seat
There's children crawling around my feet.

The surgery is nearly full by now
The sweat is running from my brow.

I start to wonder when's my turn?
Then my stomach starts to churn.

The doctors know they have the powers
To make you wait for hours and hours.

By now I'm moulded to the chair
Sweat still running through my hair.

He's called my name, my teeth are grating
Mustn't keep the doctor waiting.

I make my way along the hall
Pictures hanging on the wall.

I knock the door and go right in,
On his face there is a grin.

He sits me down and says to me,
'What can I do my son for thee?'

I tell him what I've come in for,
He gives me some pills and shows me the door.

I found my way out feeling so grim
I'm feeling worse now than when I went in!

M P Oliver

Grandparenting

You come to my house treat it like your own place
Running and shouting invading my space.
Demanding this, demanding that, I'm sure if I had one
You'd frighten the cat.
You think your voice should always be heard
And you always win word upon word.
You drop your belongings for me to pick up
You don't want a beaker, you *need that* cup.
You inspect the fridge, go through my stores
Won't leave me in peace to get on with my chores
You bully me into a game of *Snap* when really you ought
To be taking a nap.
You cuddle up close and when I ask, 'What?'
You slink away leaving me covered in snot.
You try on my glasses pretend to be me
Leave them all smudged and then I can't see.
We go to the supermarket, you think I should buy
Kids This, Kids That, for *me* to try.
You pester to help me, you pester to bake
Then stubbornly refuse to eat the cake.
You can't take a bath without soaking the floor
I'm mopping up water as far as the door.
You climb in my bed, pretend to be scared
Snore and make smells that just can't be compared.
You leave crumbs on the sofa, crumbs on the floor
Icky, sticky fingerprints all over the door.
Oh, but when you have left
Normal service resumes
The silence is dreadful in my empty rooms.

Mary Younger

WHAT'S IN A HAT?

When he was young he wore a cap
Chiefly wrong way round.
As older grew, new headgear sought
Determined, careful what he bought.
To please him hard to find.

With care he chose in courting days
When trilby hat he saw.
He thought it made him look quite dashing,
Would leave all rivals' teeth a'gnashing,
Of this he was so sure.

But when he took a city job
A bowler hat selected,
As all the former headgear worn
Including homburg proudly borne,
He, at this point, rejected.

Now he's getting on a bit
And lost most all his hair,
Indoors or out with bowler find,
(E'en in the bath if he's a mind),
His head still hatted there.

Mary Ryan

Little Willie

Little Willie, nasty boy
Broke his brother's favourite toy
Killed his hamster, stony dead
Then put maggots in his sister's bed.

All Willie's pets die within a week
He superglued the budgie's beak
Tied his dog to the back of a truck
Hung his rabbit on a butcher's hook.

Willie fought with next door's cat
Splattered it with a cricket bat
When Willie's mother asked him, 'Why?'
He said, 'I was aiming for a fly.'

His mother said, 'Sorry, he's only seven
He's promised to be good when he's in Heaven.'
The thought of Heaven turned Willie green
So he shoved mother's head through the TV screen.

M J Bentley

BATHTIME

Mum says I need a bath
But I don't think I do
I had a bath a while ago
Do I look clean to you?

Mum says I need my neck cleaned
But I don't think I do
I know there's nothing growing there
Does it look clean to you?

Mum says I need my feet washed
But I don't think I do
I think it's just a suntan
Do they look tanned to you?

Mum says I need my face scrubbed
But I don't think I do
Of course Mum knows who I am
You know it's me, don't you?

Mum says I need my hair washed
But I don't think I do
The colour hasn't changed that much
Does it look black to you?

But Mum says I need a bath
And to do as I am told
I don't mind getting in
But I always come out cold.

J L Preston

THE HALF-CROWN

Along the road
the cornfield stood
where horse-drawn reaper
flailed and threshed
the days were long
recent clouds had gone.

Yellow beams glistened, gleamed
light on heavy harvest food
the late lark departing
suddenly swiftly with second brood.

Hurrying, scurrying
the fieldmice scattered
their nests tattered, forlorn
our stalked up sheaves
midst the close growing clover
unbalanced, half topping over.

The reaper still came around
and the clock ticked slow
as the field seemed to grow
elevenses a dim, distant view.

A summer break, sunny, sublime
half-a-crown for the week
seemed a good idea
at the time!

Brian Strand

THE DOCTOR

Since I became a doctor, I earn a pile in fees,
Although I do my very best to put folk at their ease.

They may have just a common cold, a model they may be?
Perhaps an eighteen year old, then I say, 'Strip for me!'

With stethoscope I press around, my ear upon her chest
And listen to that pit-a-pat, as I hand her, her vest!

'You need a massage Miss,' I say, 'at very least twice a week,'
Opening my briefcase, for the diary I keep.

I'm pleased to say the treatment, that I applied with zest,
Has now increased twice weekly, at my client's request.

I'm not sure if the massage will really be a cure,
I do know I feel younger, with a patient so demure!

I say to her, 'Tell all your friends of the treatment you receive,
The more you introduce, of course, I shall reduce the fees.'

Dr Wilby Worthless

Wouldn't It Be Nice To Get On With My Neighbours?

Oh wouldn't it be nice to get on with my neighbours
Instead of constant rows and him hammering my door
I know she threw paint up my front door, wait till I get hold
She also smashed my window, I know cos I've been told.

'Your kids have done this, then they've done that,
They've even thrown stones at the old lady's cat.'
Some folk love causing trouble, see how far they can push
Until someone stands their ground and smacks them in the mush.

'Your kids have been playing football up against my wall,
If that ball comes in my garden, I'll run a knife through that ball.'
Why don't people get along together and let me live my life
Instead of screaming at me with one large carving knife.

Wild parties all night long, loud music blasting out
Everyone's in work tomorrow of that there is no doubt
I'd just like to get some sleep now, more than a well earned rest
Instead of blasting music that next door thinks the best.

Always doing DIY till the early hours of the morn
I don't know what's he's building, the time it's took, a baby
could've been born.
When I decide to put up a shelf or repair a loose floorboard
He'd run around from next door about the noise, there must be a law.

I complained on numerous occasions about the barking dogs
He'd let them out in the morning - go to work, the barking never
stopped
I went round one night, bought the dog off his wife for fifty quid
I let it bark in my back garden and see how my neighbour likes it.

Leigh Smart

The Day Granny Let Rip A Fart!

There we were, all dressed in our Sunday best,
With Granny at our side wearing a nest on her head.
The vicar in the pulpit was preaching a gospel
And we like good citizens purely nodded.

When all of a sudden there was a rumble like thunder
And the pulpit started to rock,
The candles on the altar started to falter
Then put themselves out.
The rumble that was getting increasingly louder,
Turned on the walls that started to shake
And the slates on the roof began to fly,
Letting the rain outside inside.

The smell that emerged was enough to kill,
Hit the vicar full force then the organist too.
The choirboys started dropping like flies,
A look of sheer terror was in their eyes.

Through all of this drama Granny sat there asleep,
Innocently unaware of the demon she'd released.

Mum gave her a nudge, then Granny awoke,
A sly little smirk enveloped Granny's face
As she surveyed the look on the vicar's face.

For 30 long years I've listened to his sermons
Love thy neighbour, turn the other cheek,
But since yesterday I've eaten all the beans
I could muster, when I found out he'd
Run my poor cat over.

So, if ever to church on a Sunday you roam,
Be wary of the Granny sitting alone,
The one with the hat that resembles a nest,
Beware her backside could be a hornets' nest.

Jane Margaret Isaac

IRENE, THE IRISH COLLEEN

The irresistible Irene was an Irish colleen
Who was pretty and very quick witted
She was in love with a man
They called Dullard Dan
But to Irene he wasn't quite fitted.

Tho' Irene was no fool this boy made her drool
And her poor little heart was a-quiver
She forgot all her learning
When she couldn't stop yearning
For Dan's kisses that just made her shiver.

In time it was plain that she'd have to refrain
From seeing her sweetheart Dan
He could kiss he could cuddle
But he got into a muddle
When he tried to behave like a man.

She tried to excite him, she'd lick and she'd bite him
But nothing she did seemed to work,
She finally admitted
To Dan she was unfitted
When he ran off with Justin, the jerk.

Valerie McKinley

PETER - AGED SEVEN YEARS

Visiting the Tower of London, first time in his life,
Full of questions about everything, speculation rife.
'What are those strange black birds,
Why do the men wear funny skirts?'
All shouted in a childish treble (it's the blatant exposure that hurts)!

Then the soldiers of the guard, on parade for the RSM,
He was fascinated by their drill, couldn't take his eyes off them.
Suddenly, as they clashed and snapped, his treble as loud as it gets -
Rang out across the parade ground, 'What are they Daddy - Cadets?'

The RSMs face contorted, but he kept himself in check.
The red tide rose so slowly up the sergeant major's neck.
You can imagine every little word the guard would hear that day!
Because of that innocent utterance, in a small child's amusing way!

J M Jones

UNTITLED

There was a boy called Bart
Who did a smelly fart
Right in the middle of our science class.

'What an odious whiff,'
said the teacher,
'What chemical did this?
Write down your answer Bart.'

Whispered Bart, 'I could win the
Nobel Prize fart.'

Alex Wilde

WILLIE STIRS IT UP

Little Willie wrote some verses
filled with naughty words and curses,
sent them to his English teacher
saying they were from the preacher.

She erupted, white with fury,
threatened priest with judge and jury -
baffled cleric, name of Percy,
dived for cover, howled for mercy.

Such a stir young Will created
local press investigated,
tabloids, broadsheets, TV too
but they didn't have a clue.

Little Willie gave a chuckle,
sent more poems 'near the knuckle';
he's a rascal, he's a menace,
worse by far than Beano's Dennis.

Sheila Burnett

THE BUNGAROO

The Bungaroo was full of goo
From a cold so bad
It filled his ear so he couldn't hear
He was oh so sad.

A tip from a friend to help him mend
He was pleased to try
'A couple of blows of your nose
Then to the goo, goodbye.'

With a big hoot and a little toot
He gave the tip a crack
The goo in his ear was finally clear
And his hearing it came back.

Andrew Younger

THE SQUATTER

Just a minute Mr Sparrow, I'd really like a word,
You are sitting in my bird box and it's upset my 'live in' bird.
We flew out for a minute to catch greenfly for our tea,
Now you've really spoilt things, it's not big enough for three!

I'm just a little blue tit - not half the size of you,
But I'll stand up for my rights and claim what is my due.
I'll see if PC Robin can move you from my nest,
Or he might just simply charge you
And let Bird Law do the rest.

We were planning for a family,
Two or three or more.
We didn't plan for sparrows
To come flying through our door!

There is something I must tell you,
So won't you come outside,
I'm not out to ruffle feathers
And I've not a thing to hide.

I've been told there is a bird box
In a tree next door,
With a 'To Let' sign on it,
So what are you waiting for?

Oh, I forgot to tell you
As you quickly flew past me,
The reason why it's empty - is,
It's the black cat's favourite tree!

Milly Hatcher

The Adventures Of Little Willie

Willie had a wooden neck,
Would he wash it, would be eck?
The problem was, his throat was dry,
This caused the wood to grow awry.

Wee Willie failed every test,
At school, he ruled as teacher's pest,
He left a tack upon her chair
And watched her bum rise in the air.

We Willie's mum was full of woe,
He left and joined the circus show,
How could he take the family pet
She missed that dog, it made her fret!

Wee Willie simply lost the plot,
The day he set the iron on hot,
He pressed his sister's head so flat,
She wears a blackboard for a hat.

Wee Willie went out with a bang,
On Guy Fawkes night the children sang,
He lit a rocket and held on
And now his name is in neon.

Pat Derbyshire/Dave Worthington (1st two lines)

LITTLE WILLIE'S

Willie's mom sent him to school
to educate the little fool,
staff and pupils joined the race
to exit him to outer space.

Aliens and heavenly folk
failed to see this earthling joke
so kicked our Will where it hurts most -
and back he came by first-class post.

To prove that he was here to stay
a shopping trip he planned - that day
he took with him his favourite cat
and went to buy his new school hat.

The traffic light showed clearly red
well - that was what a witness said,
but Willie failed to notice that
now Willie, hat and cat are flat.

Jim Pritchard

LITTLE WILLIE WAG-TAIL

Little Willie Wag-Tail
Plodding through the snow,
Little Willie Wag-Tail
Never knowing which way to go.

Little Willie Wag-Tail
Always on the move,
Little Willie Wag-Tail
What is it you wish to prove?

Little Willie Wag-Tail
What drives or motivates you so?
Little Willie Wag-Tail
Plodding through the snow.

Gary J Finlay

Church Matters

Church matters make the setting for satire and many a joke
About ministers, vicars and pastors and other less notable folk.

A scene on the theme of Jesus, the children were asked to draw
By their Sunday School teacher, encouraging participation by all.
One girl drew an aeroplane - her classmate was very surprised
'Now I'm going to draw Pontius Pilate,' she very quickly replied.

The children were really listening as the teacher tried to explain
The wisdom and foresight of Noah before it began to rain.
Then, nearing the end of the story, as the clock began to chime
She asked, 'How do you think whilst in the Ark, Noah spent his time?'
After a moment of silence she thought, prompting is needed here,
'Did he do a lot of fishing?'
'With only two worms Miss, no fear!'

A young teacher explained to the children
How Lot's wife was badly at fault
When she looked backward - that was the reason
She turned into a pillar of salt.
One little lad sat quite unimpressed
Then interrupted with a voice so droll
'That's nothing Miss - when Mother was driving,
She turned into a telegraph pole.'

The fall of Adam and Eve in the garden
Was searched by a mind quite profound
He found it was not caused by the apple,
But by the pair on the ground.
As I have now outrun my time, this must be the end of rhyme.

Greta Bray

OLDE SKOOL

I couldn't be bothered doing any work
And all of a sudden,
I went berserk,
I stood on the tabletop up high,
Spread out my arms
And pretended to fly.
I began to recite Radio Gaga by Queen,
The poor student teacher
Had never watched such a scene.
At the front I danced the YMCA,
By this point the teacher,
Didn't know what to say.
Rules and regulations mattered no more,
Because groovy boy Danny,
Was on the floor!
In came the head teacher and that's where the fun ends
And here on my bottom
Is where the cane mark bends.

Daniel C Wright

DOUBLE VISION

There was a young man called John
Who refused to put his glasses on.
Contact lenses were what he preferred
So to the optician he was referred.
Now there's one thing he had to remember to do,
At the end of the day, flush his lenses down the loo.
Poor John he awoke one morning
Feeling misty-eyed as the day was dawning.
From the packet new lenses he did take
And put in his eyes, not realising his mistake!
Suddenly everything was out of focus
As he stumbled over things he woke us.
The day continued to get worse
He felt sure it was a wretched curse.
So he went early to bed,
With a very sore head.
As he remembered the optician's advice,
Removing his lenses felt nice.
With a flick of his finger, he aimed for the bin
And to his horror, found for the day, he'd had two pairs in.

Annette Murphy

GAMBLER

A man's wife found a woman's name in his pocket
She quizzed him when he returned from work
'It's a horse that runs like a rocket.'
As he turned around with a smirk
She believed him this time like many before
But still had doubts in her head
It plagues her all night as she thought much more
As she tosses and turns in her bed
Next day when he returned from the cold
His wife flattened his nose with a bang.
'What was that for?' as he stood there so bold.
'As if you don't know, your horse rang.'

Ray Stuart

Poor Mr Bond

Now poor Mr Bond
Fell into the pond
And found he couldn't swim
He started to shout
When he couldn't get out
And that was the end of him.

Jean McGovern

TOM, JERRY AND BARRY

The barrel chest let out a mighty roar
Shivering, Tom skittered across the floor.
'Please,' he whimpered, 'I'm just a kitten,
To fight with me would hardly be fitting.'
Barry the bulldog increased his pace
With a great big grin on his ugly face.
'Help me God, if I've been naughty,
It's because Jerry's so haughty.'
With seconds to spare, he spied Jerry's hole
Slithered through like a practised mole.
Landed splashing in his own puddle,
Shaking, quaking, all of a huddle.
He heard a squeak, saw Jerry take a leap
'Won't hurt you Jerry, this promise I'll keep.
That bulldog was shocking, let us be friends,
A reformed character, I'll make amends.
We'll live in harmony you and me
We can be buddies, just wait and see.'
Yes, promises are easy to make
Wise Jerry that advice wouldn't take.
He tweaked the cat's tail, to Tom's chagrin,
The victor at last, such jubilation.
Sweet music hearing old Tom plead
Barry would be mightily pleased.

Kathleen Potter

RIOTOUS GREAT-GRANDMA

Today I'm in a festive mood
So let it now be understood,
By all and sundry, my design
For a long life is to drink wine
With all my meals; and in-between,
A 'little something' I esteem.
So here's to us: The Best of British!
And now, while I am feeling skittish
For ageing I don't care a fig -
To make my point, I'll dance a jig!

Evelyn Westwood

A SIMPLE FAULT

Why won't you do this simple task
That's all I ask of you?
I have followed all the instructions
From one to twenty-two.

I have checked all your connections
I've replaced your fuses too.
But still there is no sign of life
What else can I do?

I hate these things called computers
It was working one hour ago.
I only stopped for a cup of tea
While the wife could Hoover through.

Hang on, I've just thought of something
Which wall plug did she use?
Aha, there's the problem
That why my computer's got no juice.

With the plug switched on at the socket
A picture suddenly appears.
I just don't fancy doing it now
I'll go for a couple of beers!

John Gwynne

Molly The Mower

Fill her with fuel, get ready to go,
Molly the Mower, my best friend or foe?
One pull at the rip-chord is sometimes enough,
If it is damp, she goes cough, choke and snuff.

Bring down to start, then pull and begin,
Open the choke and then pull once again;
Suddenly, out comes a big cloud of dust,
She shudders, then off with a throb and a thrust.

Pull down the lever for fast forward speed,
Then run to keep up with this galloping steed;
She goes tearing away and mounts up the bank,
Old Molly the Mower is just like a tank.

Front lawns are finished, now round to the back,
Past the stone steps and the flowers in the rack;
Up to the orchard and down to the lane,
Molly the Mower must be mad or insane!

Norma Rudge

CAT'S EYE VIEW

What right has she to talk like that?
To say the floor's my place!
Can't help it if my fur comes out
And sometimes I have fleas.

To send a guest out in the cold
Whenever food's about!
And not to let me go upstairs
To share her warmth in bed!

In former days now I was fed
As often as I asked.
This woman says two meals a day
Is all I'm going to get!

I must confess I'm much more fit
Than I have ever been.
I pounce on palpitating mice,
Young birds and long-nosed shrews.

Now the night is clear and still;
That woman's calling me.
I'm not prepared to go indoors,
This hunter's not a pet!

Pamela Sanders

The Story Of Pat

Now Pat she was a pretty wife with curls all tossed and wild;
And life was very sunny until she had another child.
With her husband only working and the other child made four;
The money had been stretched so far, it couldn't stretch no more.

With the cost of living rising and money value going down;
It wasn't so surprising Pat could only sit and frown.
Till she hit on a solution; put the kettle on the hob,
She was only twenty-two now, she would go and find a job.

So she looked up all the adverts, picked a number, gave a ring,
Sure a part time shop assistant, was just the very thing.
They talked of hours of working and discussed the rates of pay;
Then she heard the voice upon the line say, 'Good, start right away.'

When she got a baby sitter, she showered, powdered and
scrubbed clean.
She was the prettiest, little housewife that you have ever seen.
Now the supervisor was surprised that she should start that very day,
But the boss had gone away for lunch and didn't even say.

Though he was so absent-minded that no one made a fuss.
As Pat took off her coat and gloves and put away her purse.
She wrapped up parcels, gave out change, she was so smart, serene,
That the supervisor did admit, she was the best he'd ever seen.

Until the boss returned from lunch and Pat heard him calling, *'Stop!*
There must be some mistake, this cannot be the shop.
I don't need a shop assistant and that's the truth, my sweet,
I'll bet you've been employed by the wee shop down the street.'

Bridie Taber Beeson

UNTITLED

Willie was a naughty boy,
Thought his pet was just a toy
He dunked it in the river,
Didn't see the poor pet shiver;
Didn't listen to its plaintive cry,
Just pegged it on the line to dry.

Little Willie wished he was a girl,
Put on a frock and gave a twirl.
Minced down the road, then got mad!
He was chased, caught and *kissed,* by a *lad!*

Little Willie had a heart of gold,
But would never do what he was told.
Playing with fire he soon learned,
That way, his house and toys were *burned!*

Hazel M Birch

UNTITLED

Willie and his friends did play,
Having great fun on the way.
Stones were hitting everyone,
Said, 'Just Willie having fun.'

Little Willie, firework day,
Chances many came his way.
Lit Sparklers, put inside girls' frocks,
Great to see them scream and hop.

Barbara Goode

UNTITLED

Little Willie's in a jam,
Tried to board a moving tram.
Seedless Raspberry, says the label
Gives me the willies on the table!

Little Willie in a paddy
Grabbed a gun and shot his daddy.
Mother in a frightful strop
Cried, 'William, this has got to stop!'

Maureen & George Carr

LITTLE WILLIE - ON THE LEVEL

Little Willie, canny creep,
Did kiss a girl and make her weep;
Tears they trickled and I'll tell you why,
Willie munched an onion 'fore he pecked her in the eye.

Little Willie, naughty knave,
Did ask a corpse, 'Why art thou so . . . grave?'
'Respect,' barked a mourner, 'for the dearly departed!'
Willie, as the Cockneys say, upped and apple-tarted.

Little Willie, thorough thug,
Pinched a pair of antique jugs,
Held them aloft in joyous suspension,
The owner she moaned (for she liked the attention).

Little Willie, tricky thing,
Helped himself to a maiden's ring,
Asleep was she, so he did not linger,
This glistening band sat well on his finger.

Little Willie, beastly boy,
Stole a housewife's favourite toy,
In church it caused a fair old buzz,
Smooth lil' Will don't get caught by the fuzz.

Little Willie, fiendish felon,
Squeezed the grocer's watermelons,
She told him straight, 'Pay for what you paw!'
So he nibbled her raspberries and left the store.

Little Willie, on the loose,
He'll pilfer your morellos then give you a goose,
How do I know this rogue runs free?
Little Willie . . . I am he!

Jon Oyster

LITTLE WILLIES

Little Willie hates his father,
Says he really would much rather
Have a dog that he could love,
Then he'd give his dad the shove.

Little Willie is a pain,
Into trouble once again.
Caused a lot of aggravation,
Court have put him on probation.

Little Willie has a double,
Both of them are causing trouble.
Willie goes off scrumping fruit,
T'other promptly follows suit.

Willie went and shopped with Mother,
Naturally he caused some bother.
When she went to pay the bill
He pinched some money from the till.

Little Willie's had enough,
All this talk of 'brother love'.
If he's allowed to have his way
He'd drown him in the River Tay.

Willie's New Year resolution
Is increase atmosphere pollution,
In the garden lighting fires
Burning lots of worn-out tyres.

Little Willie is life's bane,
Drives his mother, near insane.
Told to eat his breakfast up
He spills his milk and breaks his cup.

Willie is a likely lad,
Sometimes good but often bad.
Par for course you learn is when
The ratio is one to ten.

Little Willie drives me wild,
Cannot someone curb the child?
Father made the rascal wail
When he pulled the pussy's tail.

Willie in the swimming pool,
Messed about and played the fool.
Vicar's daughter he abhorred,
So pushed her off the diving board.

Tony Channon

The Vicar's Daughter

A young vicar's lass from Dundee
Drank gallons and gallons of tea,
Whilst walking her dog, she stepped . . on a frog
Then hopped in a field . . . for a wee!

But unknown to her . . . whilst squatting there
The frog's family they did gather.
They stared at the sight . . . and with croaks of delight
Decided to put her on TV.

Camcorder in hand, Grandfather Froggy did stand,
He recorded the whole sordid scene
Thinking . . . (Yes, I have caught her, the vicar's daughter)
Doing what he'd think obscene.

The case came to court . . . evidence was produced,
Both froggies and vicar stood firm,
Neither prepared to give just an inch,
But there was a lesson to learn.

Her lawyer refused to accept the proof; the froggie family hit the roof,
Jumping in unison . . . as high as they could,
Croaking, 'But the vicar's daughter never should
Have squashed poor Freddie cos he wasn't ready, to leave his family'

A smirk appeared . . . . on the judge's face,
He'd decided there was no case.
No matter how loud the plaintiffs did scream,
His opinion was, this had all been a bad dream.

Because one of his cases . . . the day before,
Was about a hedgehog that had been run o'er.
His wife was involved in that incident
So inwardly thinking? Was this Heaven-sent?

She had had a drink of port . . . er!
Maybe the same happened to the vicar's daughter!

Who knows the truth of this storey?
Be it a dream . . . or a fantasy?
Drinking and driving do not mix
Frogs and hedgehogs end up in a ditch.

Not been missed by some human beings,
But, surely froggies and hedgies, do have feelings!

Pensioner Pam

THE DIDGERIDOO THAT DIDN'T DO

There once was a didgeridoo
Who didn't know quite what to do.
Its owner found, it made no sound
However long he blew.
He said growing red in the face
'I think you're a perfect disgrace,
So if it's the last thing I do
I'll get a sound out of you.'
But the didgeridoo couldn't,
Or the didgeridoo wouldn't
Do what it was supposed to do.
Said its owner in bed that night,
'I must try to get things right
If my didgeridoo won't play
I'll have to give it away
And play with my new kangaroo.'
He then changed its name
And thus it became
The didgeri-didn't do!
The didgeridoo didn't like it
He thought it would never do,
So he removed something shocking
That he discovered was blocking
The tube of his didgeridoo.
    Oh you stupid didgeridoo
    Causing all that hullabaloo!

Margaret Nixon

UNTITLED

Little Willie, such a jerk.
Cut off the cat's tail to see it work.
It wagged twice and then it died.
Said Mum, 'I hope you're satisfied.'

Willie found an electric guitar.
The noise could be heard from afar.
Until his mum turned him into a rocket
By sticking his finger into the socket.

Linda Ann Johnson

WEE WILLIE

Wee Willie and mother went to park
for a lark
got on the swing
high kick and fling.

Wee Willie came down
he nearly broke his crown
with a cross frown
Mother shouted Willie get off the ground.

Wee Willie went down the slide
he turned and landed on his side
knocked into another boy's back
Mother screamed *Willie* you no knack.

Wee Willie went on roundabout
children scream and shout
Willie has us in a spin
Mother says *Willie* stop the din.

Marie Coyles

LITTLE WILLIE AND THE BULL

Little Willie went to a farm,
He didn't mean to do no harm!
But he opened in one field, a gate
He didn't realise what would be his fate.

Willie entered the field, so bold
He never did as he was told,
Not caring, he didn't bother to shut the gate
And didn't see the bull 'til it was too late!

The great fat beast came bearing down,
The road out the field led down to town,
So the bull just tore on into the street
Trampling over all the poor people's feet.

Talk about a bull in a china shop!
He went right on and didn't stop,
That's when Willie came running along,
But what could he do, he's not that strong.

Willie got in the way of the bull
To try and stop him, what a fool!
He got more than squashed toes and a bleeding head,
I'm afraid to say poor Willie's dead!

Jane Otieno

LITTLE WILLIE'S . . .

Little Willie's not so good
On his sister's shoulders stood
Nothing wrong with that you said
He was only kicking his sister's head!

Found a bottle he thought lemonade
Didn't know it was a hand grenade
Saw the pin, pulled it out,
Little Willie, now is nowt!

W E Clements

LITTLE WILLIE

Little Willie found a cat,
He sat it on the bedroom mat.
He fixed it to some dynamite,
And watched it shoot into the night!

Little Willie was eating jelly,
He ate so much it filled his belly.
More and more he would not stop,
Until his belly just went pop!

Little Willie hated school,
He thought his teacher was a ghoul.
One day he set her skirt alight,
And laughed to see her in such fright!

Little Willie was playing ball,
It hit him hard and he did fall.
For weeks and weeks his eye was black,
And never again did he go back!

Little Willie was on his bike,
He met his sister on a hike.
He sent her rolling down the hill,
Just like poor old Jack and Jill!

Little Willie was up a tree,
He needed to go and have a wee.
Poor little boy could not get down,
And little Willie's pants turned brown!

Elizabeth Holt (13)

POOR WILLIE

Little Willie, sent to bed,
Thought he'd take a walk instead,
Found the night was black as pitch,
Fell into a muddy ditch.

Reluctant pupil at his school,
Will stood upon the dunce's stool,
Peashooter primed, took careful aim.
One splendid shot! - but end of game.

On a plank Will went to sea,
Vowing he'd a pirate be,
Sink ships, make captives walk the plank.
Alas! 'Twas Willie's plank that sank.

Willie wanted to discover
If his mother had a lover,
To the keyhole pressed his ear.
Said Mother, 'You'll get earache, dear.'

Willie tried to milk a cow,
Though he didn't quite know how.
He placed the bucket near her tail.
It wasn't milk that filled the pail!

Skateboarding Willie made more noise
Than all the other noisy boys.
Yet silence reigned when he was found.
He'd skated on a pond and drowned.

V E Godfrey

To The Dentist

To the dentist we hate to go
Because he hurts us as you know,
He says, 'Open your mouth and let me see
Oh you must have some out,' and out comes three.

He says, 'I've taken the wrong ones out
But never mind just hang about
I'll take three more for sure
At least you won't have to worry about them anymore.'

'Well, I'll make you another plate.'
But to have false teeth I would hate,
I suppose it is better than being gummy
And I would look very funny.

He pushed and stretched my mouth so wide
To see if he could get inside,
'Get out you nasty man
It's false teeth I'll have not your hand.'
And now I have a gleaming pair
Of teeth which I'll have to wear.

Joy Hall

A Riddle

A little dot on the paper
here's the plot, not a caper.
What is the nature of this cause?
Try again and do not pause.
Find the dot and do the deed
that is all you will need.
Now that you have got the answer
tell it to me, are you a chancer?
If you are and know the plot
then you will be able to find the dot.

Niall McManus

LIMERICK

There was a young lady from Sale,
Who bought a black cat with no tail;
She asked it, 'Manx?'
The cat said, 'No thanks,
I'd prefer a portion of whale!'

Muriel Willa

Missus Moneybags: Two Thousand And Two

Now I have been accused of late
For extreme jealousy concerning the fate
Of a domestic I employed for a while
She laid it on thick, with a coquettish smile

John dear, my best friend
Became so enamoured: I sensed friendship's end
But I chose to try to ameliorate
What had become of this lady's fate

She was very good looking, on a good day,
And she wanted a rich man to help assay
The hardships and loneliness she was in:
He offered the chance of living in sin

Now, me here, now that I'm past all that sort of panky
Couldn't understand why she waved her hankie:
Was it in sorrow or triumph she departed
Can't say I was exactly broken-hearted

Oh my dears, if you could believe
What airs and graces she felt she'd achieved:
Her new man, middle-age itch, still obviously liked his little bit -
Wasn't true what she said: she'd rather have a cup of tea than go to bed

Oh, he liked his desserts that's for sure:
She said it was over quick and satisfying, what's more:
She asked of me once, a terribly curious question to my mind:
I didn't chose to ask if her man would hold his erection:
I merely became resigned.

With her slender frame and blonded hair
She was Mrs Success whilst I alas, was Ms Despair:
Had a terrible time you see with a local hairdresser
Had to have all my long hair off - it was ruined beyond repair.

So I add, as a rider, be careful, who mounts you, like Keeler -
Whilst she was up to her neck in champagne,
Profumo was up to his b**ls in cider, trying to ride her . . .

Joy Sheridan

Revolting Rhymes

While dining out, don't send back your tea,
however horrible it may be.
Whatever replaces it
may well contain someone's spit.
Just don't tip - and smile disdainfully.

As you spoon in the food on your tray
relaxing after a stressful day
a doctor on the TV
slices someone you can see -
and you have to push your plate away.

Chris Creedon

The Things Men Do To Drive You Up The Wall

Men definitely have habits that drive you up the wall
leaving things around waiting for you to fall
always leaving a sink of pots
leaving mess on the mirror after squeezing their spots
they never lift the toilet seat when taking a pee
scratching their bums in public for everyone to see
walking through the house with muddy feet
oil filled trousers as they sit in your seats
you can depend on them to leave stubble in your sink
five minutes to wash away if only they would think
why do we clean after them in every way
there should be a way to make them pay.

A Boyes

TRIVIAL

Would that life were simple,
Alas it is not so.
For every hill surmounted
There's hundreds more to go!
Round every corner, a surprise
Seldom to one's liking,
Speeding ever onward,
Losing grip and sliding
Into the mire of life!

Sarah Allison

RELATED DREAMS

I am the dream you
Never had twice -
You never forgot and
Was ever so nice

The person I brought you
Was unknown before -
But not now I'll wager
Though you don't know her door!

For I am the dream
You never told mother,
Fiancé or wife - but
You did tell your brother

Who smiled, I'll bet knowingly -
And said,
'Here's another' -
And brought you my father-in-law.

Peter Asher

SUNDAY'S BOOTSALE

I'm wondering how many will be selling at the
Bootsale this Sunday? Probably quite a few.
Some will know what their items are worth,
Others won't have a clue.

I won't be seeking anything in particular
Maybe something that just takes my fancy.
A book or something collectable
Perhaps a jug for Aunty Nancy.

Every stallholder has a tale to tell
About the pieces on their table.
Some of which may be true,
Or possibly just another fable.

How much is the painting?
A voice shouts from the crowd.
Make me an offer quick
As I don't like the look of that black cloud.

Money changes hands faster than I could ever count it
All kinds of tempting offers here
I like that new tool kit.

I've had a look around, nothing has really caught my eye.
I think I'll make my way home now,
Just look at the colour of that sky.

Phillip Walters

Little Willie

Little Willie, don't you know
Tripped and spilt his grandma's po,
Though the carpet's ruined now,
Will stood up and took a bow.

Will, the porridge, thought he'd made,
Ended up an oatmeal cake,
Sliced it up and served with tea
He's taken orders now for three.

Little Willie mowed the lawn,
O'er the flowerbed, now it's gone,
Mother scolded at his deeds
Now he's out there planting seeds.

Willie climbed a tree one day,
Sun was hidden, clouds were grey,
Started raining, just like that
Will 'rived home as drowned as rat.

Little Willie stayed in bed,
Started sneezing, cold in head,
While he's doing not a thing
Mother treats him like a king.

Little Willie's back at school
Studies hard, yet acts the fool,
And though he doesn't know it yet,
He has been named 'teacher's pet'.

Colin Ross

PAST TIMES

Willie loves to sew and stitch,
But finding things to mend's a hitch.
So he has to cut and slash
And then repairs things in a flash.

Willie has no sense of shape
And body parts all tend to gape.
Arms are where the legs should be
And eyes don't have the chance to see.

Ivy Jones

I Think I Thunk

Some things are too complex for me.
Who can believe electricity?
I've no belief in pie in the sky,
or things that occur in an elephant's eye,
and certainly not that planes can fly.
The only things that are plain to me
are those I can distinctly see.
Radio has to be total fiction -
I believe in TV but that's my addiction.
Everything else is so much bunk -
at least that's what I think, I thought, I thunk.

W Ballantyne Scott

CHOCOHOLIC

I admit I'm a chocoholic
I know many others too
Who cannot eat one bar of chocolate
Without taking another one or two.
If there's a box of chocolate in the house
Then I'll sit and munch them all night
So I don't wonder why my clothes don't fit
Why all the waistbands are too tight.
There's just something about chocolate
I can drool just mentioning it
If I wasn't so addicted
Then I'd only eat a tiny bit.
Although I suffer from migraine
And I cannot touch cheese or wine
I can eat a box of chocolate
And still be feeling fine.
So chocoholics of the world unite
Just stop dreaming and take another bite.

Mary Anne Scott

BUSES

My bus leaves at 4.30.
I arrive at twenty past
To make sure I don't miss it.
(Well, I can't run very fast.)

I check my watch - 4.30,
It should be here very soon.
Oh great! It's started raining now!
(My brolly is at home.)

I want the Maidstone bus today.
The listings say they run
At twenty minute intervals.
(Except when I want one!)

I come to the conclusion
That the bus I want is 'off'.
That's *another* twenty minutes
Standing, waiting at the stop!

Whatever bus you're waiting for,
Where e'er you're going to,
The ones you *don't* want all turn up
In droves and smirk at you!

I've been here for an hour now!
I'm soaked and want my tea!
Ah - here it comes at last!
I don't believe it, look, there's three!

Anne Gardiner

Oceans Of Notions

How many poems does a man have to write
Before they call him a poet?
How many rivers does a man have to cross
Before they give him a new boat?
The answer my friend is rowing in the wind,
The answer is rowing in the wind.
How many lives does a cat have left
When he has been killed nine times?
None I would say, he has had his day,
He has gone, he is done and that rhymes.
The answer my friend is mewing in the wind,
The answer is mewing in the wind.
How many swallows make a summer?
More than one I would venture to say.
How many snowflakes would cover the land
On a cold, dark winter's day?
The answer my friend is flying in the wind,
The answer is flying in the wind.

T F Ryan

BABY TALK

You might think it funny
Stuck out here with nothing but a dummy
To keep me company,
Lying here with a soaking nappy
Cold and hungry too!
Come and get me, there's a good mum
Put a clean diaper on my bum
Then I'll stop crying!
Let me see a sight of that nipple
Promising me an hour-long tipple
What a lovely thought!
Pooh, I say, what an awful smell
I must have done the other job as well -
Hope Mum's in a good mood!

M Trussler

GROWING UP

Being a baby, is not for me,
Can't do a thing for yourself
Father bounces you on his knee,
It makes me feel sick
Why can't they leave you be?
I object to being manhandled
To watch some cartoons on TV,
Let's change the channels quick.

Being a toddler can be a strain,
This toddling makes my legs ache
I keep falling over, again and again,
Can they not carry me?
You hurt yourself so you cry with pain,
Just looking for sympathy
Mum takes you out shopping, in the rain,
Oh! What glee.

Being at nursery just gives me stress,
Rather stay at home
I get dragged there daily nonetheless,
Girls should be banned
It gives Mum time to herself I guess,
Me too
Thank goodness she returns I confess,
Phew, thought I was orphaned.

Being in primary, what an awful fate
This is no picnic
Most days we hurry because we're late,
It's not because of me
For the last bell I can hardly wait,
Freedom
I'm always first out the school gate,
Let's get home for tea.

Being at high school, that's a drag,
Too much homework
We hide in the toilets to have a fag,
Not getting one's a crisis
Our art teacher's a lonely old bag,
She isn't really
In history we learned about the Reichstag,
Haven't got a clue what that is.

Being grown-up and working hard
Wish I could win the lottery
It's not easy in the dockyard,
No chance of promotion here
Would I have done better as a guard?
We'll never know
I think my whole life was marred,
Can't change it now I fear.

George S Johnstone

BIG TROUBLE . . .

That's the trouble with gardens, they get out of hand
Then you have to start slashing them back.
But the minute you stop, the weeds shoot once again
And prize flowers they once more hijack.
You chastise them severely, it's to no avail
So in temper you give them a *thwack!*
Losing your patience you wrench plants from beds
And they're all of them given the sack . . .

Crazy paving's the next thing, instead of a lawn,
No jungle's left standing to hack.
There's a place to sit snugly and while away time
And you don't have to try to keep track
Of seasons for planting or pruning and such -
Gardening books lie unread in my shack.

Blast! New weeds have run rampant among all the slabs,
Just sitting I've grown much too slack.
I'm fed up as well for there's nothing to do
So the paving I'm going to attack.
Such a brilliant idea, so I thought at the time -
Certain charm though it now seems to lack!

Different seeds that I've bought surreptitiously
Are hidden high up on a rack.
I'll sow them all neatly like garden books tell,
They'll grow beautifully now I've changed tack.
I've decided to enter some gardening shows
For I'm going to give veggies a crack.

Come on now, it's D-Day, I'm sure the time's right -
Oh no! Carrots and tatties are black.
The wife's laughed fit to bust, thinks it's funny she does,
If she's not careful I'll give her a smack!
So she's won, I give up, gardening's finished for me,
There are no more plants left to unpack.
Mother Nature can live here and do as she likes,
She's the dame with the green-fingered knack!

Paddy Jupp

UNTITLED

A lady who lives next to me
Gave birth and she had three.
Her husband named Jack
Said 'Put them all back,
None of then look like me!'

L Newcombe

Rugby Widows

It's two o'clock on a Saturday afternoon,
The crowd are singing way out of tune,
It's raining hard and I'm frozen to the bone
What am I doing here? I want to go home!

At last the players come running out,
The women wolf whistle, wink and shout,
the men flex their muscles and puff out their chests,
It's more like a Mr Universe contest!

The ref comes on in black and white,
The men are ready and waiting to fight,
The whistle blows, the ball flies high,
Now is it called a goal, or is it a try?

The hormones run high among the crowd,
A gaggle of girls are shouting out loud,
The women watch, drooling at all the men,
They'll have dropped their knickers by five past ten!

The men are bloody, cut and bruised
If this is entertainment then I'm confused!
What am I doing here? Who knows?
Thank God that the final whistle blows.
My man limps off with a glint in his eye,
He's happy, he scored the final try!

The women flock to the pub in anticipation
That the evening will end in fornication.
The laughter gets louder, the drink flows quick
The scrum half's in the corner, groaning, being sick.
Inhibitions lost, the party's begun,
I might hate rugby - but this is fun!

Heather Boyce

WATCH OUT! WATCH OUT! WILLIE'S ABOUT

Little Willie chased by a bull
Couldn't run fast, his pockets were full,
So he poked the bull in the rear,
Wicked Willie just shows no fear.

Willie then made a big lasso,
As it twirled he lassoed his shoe,
But jerking it hard to get free
Willie was left dangling from a tree.

The bull saw Willie, charged the tree
But his horns got stuck so solidly,
The tree fell down, crashed to the ground,
Airborne Willie couldn't be found.

Willie landing in a nest of ants
Crawling around, ants in his pants.
Firemen then came, doused him all day
Sun-baked Willie, like a piece of clay.

Willie fishing with a big net,
But they haven't found Willie yet,
His net was caught up in a boat,
He's down the river, all afloat.

Little Willie could not be seen,
People at last sent for the marines,
Will then suddenly appeared
Crowd applauding, then they cheered.

Little Willie just hasn't a care
But if you see him, just beware,
He's now quite famous, super brat
He does no wrong, no matter what.

Irene Grahame

HORRIBLE WILLIE

We didn't know where his sister went,
When Willie covered her in cement,
Though a statue on the patio,
Looks like a girl we used to know.

Willie is lovely when he is smiling,
All creatures find him so beguiling.
Puppies run to give him a lick,
Then he hits them with a stick.

Willie said, 'I'm going to start
To make a moving work of art.'
He covered his sister in red gloss pain,
She moves a bit but art she ain't.

In the kitchen a strange smell lingers,
Little Willie is frying fingers,
They are not fish ones Willie blisters,
Sad to say they are his little sister's.

Leo Robinson

UNTITLED

Little Willie like to tease,
Made his baby sister sneeze.
Shoved the pepper pot up her nose
Just to see how far it goes.

Naughty Willie made a bet,
To bury his sister while she slept.
Now Willie's folks are in a tiz,
Willie won't tell them where she is.

Little Willie wants a drink,
So he climbs into the kitchen sink.
Puts his tongue up the tap,
He's stuck there now - the silly chap.

Deanna L Dixon

Little Willie

Willie in one of his best new sashes,
Fell in the fire and got burnt to ashes.
Presently the room grew chilly,
'Cause no one cared to poke poor Willie!

Doris Pullen

ANCHOR BOOKS SUBMISSIONS INVITED

SOMETHING FOR EVERYONE

ANCHOR BOOKS GEN - Any subject, light-hearted clean fun, nothing unprintable please.

THE OPPOSITE SEX - Have your say on the opposite gender. Do they drive you mad or can we co-exist in harmony?

THE NATURAL WORLD - Are we destroying the world around us? What should we do to preserve the beauty and the future of our planet - you decide!

All poems no longer than 30 lines.
Always welcome! No fee!
Plus cash prizes to be won!

Mark your envelope (eg *The Natural World)*
And send to:
Anchor Books
Remus House, Coltsfoot Drive
Peterborough, PE2 9JX

OVER £10,000 IN POETRY PRIZES TO BE WON!

Send an SAE for details on our New Year 2003 competition!-